Lüde, Crüde and Rüde
The story of
Mötley Crüe

BY SYLVIE SIMMONS AND MALCOLM DOME

Published by Castle Communications Plc
Book Division, A29 Barwell Business Park
Leatherhead Road, Chessington, Surrey KT9 2NY

Copyright © 1994 Castle Communications Plc

Acknowledgments
Sylvie and Malcolm wish to thank the following people
for their help and support on this book:
Doug Thaler and Stephanie Gurevitz, Top Rock Management
Amanda Williams at WEA Records • Arlett Vereecke • Dave Ling
Skarlet at Kerrang! • Phil Scott • PG Tips (where's our sponsorship?)
And of course Mötley Crüe (where are our platinum discs?!)

Design: Brian Burrows
Picture Research: Kay Rowley

ISBN 1 898141 95 9

3

Contents

Prölögue – by Sylvie Simmons

Sunset Boulevard is empty now. The ozone layer is slowly growing back over LA There was a time when the Sunset Strip smelled like a hairdresser's from hell, a time when you could stroll the five minute stretch from Gazzarri's to the Whisky A Go Go and run into at least four hundred anorexics in painted-on pants, half a ton of Max Factor and enormous hair tortured and sprayed into oxygen-eating edifices – and that was just the boys. Now, when anyone with hair and lipstick has broken up, cleaned up or packed up and moved to Seattle, all that's left are thousands of staples stuck in the trunks of palm trees where fly posters advertising the next club date by Mötley Crüe or some look-alike band with two XXs in its name used to be. The glam scene – the tarty, party, gloriously over-the-top metal scene that dominated the '80s with its brainless babes in jacuzzis and Steven Tyler Barbie-doll boys – started here, in Los Angeles, and Mötley Crüe were its gods.

Let's put this in context. As the '80s rolled around, American metal was more like plastic. It was as flabby, wrinkled, wet and money-conscious as a middle-aged accountant in a hot tub – so sterile you could perform operations on it, so smooth you could play snooker on it, so sweet and safe and gooey that McDonalds could put it in a paper cup and sell it as a milkshake. In Britain we had the New Wave Of British Heavy Metal, but in the US Wimp Rock ruled.

Then, one night, must have been autumn '81 – I was living in LA then, writing for *Sounds* – I was outside a club called the Starwood, propped in the gutter, and I saw an apparition: 50, maybe, pale and wasted guys and girls waiting to get in, with black-lined eyes, red lips, black and white striped spandex, scarves, stilettos and layered poodle-cuts, like the New York Dolls had died and gone to hell.

I remember crawling inside. There was a cheap, tacky stage, like a giant cornflakes packet painted, like the crowd, in black and white. And on the stage were four men who looked like art-wrecko angels, like male hookers in paradise, like their audience only more so – feet stilettoed, legs spandexed or sprayed in leather, chests fishnetted T-shirts slashed to the belly-button, and topping the lot like the cherry on a cake, massive Eiffel Towers, Notre Dame Cathedrals of hair. Three blue-black, one bleached-blond. They were flash, trash and tarty. So was their music. Imagine Kiss, Sweet, biker maniacs The Godz and Alice Cooper chopped up with red-hot razor blades and played through a waste-disposal.

Their name was Mötley Crüe. They didn't have a record deal – are you kidding? No new band in LA had a record deal unless they had short hair, a thin tie and played nice new wave pop. Mötley Crüe weren't nice. They were delinquent.

9

Chapter One – In The Beginning

Let's go back just a bit. It's January '81. The best selling 'metal' albums in the States are by Foreigner and Journey, and REO Speedwagon whingeing about the vocalist's wife's marital infidelities. Frank Carlton Serafino Ferrano, aka Nikki Sixx, has left London – the band, not the place. Nikki, who came from Seattle before it was 'Seattle' and stole his first guitar at 14 so he could sell it and run away to Hollywood, was bass player with the LA band which would have been famous for featuring Blackie Lawless of WASP, only WASP wasn't born and Blackie certainly wasn't famous yet, (despite spending five minutes in the New York Dolls, a band whose music London emulated). When London decided to jump on the bandwagon and go new wave, Nikki left.

A mutual friend introduces Nikki to Thomas Lee Bass, who despite his name is a drummer. Born in Athens, Tommy Lee moved with his Greek mother and US military father to LA's San Fernando Valley when he was three years old. When Nikki found him he was playing in a band called Suite 19. Together they form a band called Christmas. But Christmas, as we all know, doesn't last. Soon after they're looking for something new. Leafing through *The Recycler* – the LA classified-ads magazine that sells everything from second-hand mattresses to musicians – they come across an ad placed by Bob Deal, a guitarist who moved to LA from Terre Haute, Indiana, and had been playing in a number of local "crummy covers bands". The ad says, simply: "loud, rude, aggressive guitarist available". Nikki and Tommy go to check him out.

"We opened the door," says Nikki, in their first interview with Sylvie for then major British rock weekly *Sounds* at the end of '81, "and we looked at each other and it was like 'Hey! What kind of hair dye do you use?!' You rarely saw people with blue-black hair and that particularly outrageous image any more. It was great!" Bob joins the band as lead guitarist; he changes his name to Mick Mars. They decide they want a rhythm guitarist. Tommy says there's a great one name of James Alverson in a band called Rock Candy. They go down to The Starwood to check him out.

The late great Starwood used to be on the corner of Crescent Heights and Santa Monica Boulevard in West Hollywood, just as it butts onto Boy's Town. Everyone played there – all the big British new wave acts did gigs there when they came to town, The Jam, The Clash, The Specials, Elvis Costello – from the sublime to the ridiculous, and everyone hung out there, from the sublime to the ridiculous too, the former getting served by waitresses in the VIP section upstairs and the latter bumming beers off visiting Valley girls on the sticky dance floor below. Which is exactly what the Crüe are doing on April Fool's Day 1981, the night they first clap eyes on Vince Neil Wharton.

Vince was a Valley boy (from the San Fernando Valley, the suburb north of the Hollywood Hills). Rock Candy, "a kind of teenybop band", as he put it, was a favourite with Valley girls. He was the singer, a candy-lipsticked glam surfer boy with bleached platinum hair.

"It was Tommy's idea to go to the Starwood to see the guitar player in the band," says Nikki. "And he's going, 'This guitarist's great!', not saying anything about Vince at all." And he certainly knew Vince. They went to the same high school in the Valley and were in rival high school bands. "But Mick really took a liking to him. We all did." But they'd already given the job of vocalist two days ago to a guy named O'Dean. "We weren't really looking for a singer," says Nikki.

"But I was," says Mick. "I didn't dig that other guy. He was at least 50lbs overweight." Unlike Vince, a total floozie, Bardot with an umlaut. The rhythm guitar player was forgotten. So was O'Dean.

So now they have their line-up, they have their songs – Nikki has been writing new material for the past year; their only cover in the early days is 'Tonight' by The Raspberries – and, courtesy of Mick Mars, they have their name. "One of my bass player friends from the band I was in, we were all sitting around – this was in '77 – he comes in and goes, 'This is a motley looking crew', and I said, 'I'm having that name for a band'." They certainly were a motley looking crew. Like a skeletal Sweet after extensive cosmetic surgery and a weekend wrestling bag ladies at fetish sex costume shop the Pleasure Chest. "Everybody can't look like Motörhead, you know," says Vince. "That," says Nikki, "takes a lot of doing." "We find the weirdest things to wear," says Vince. "Anything. We see something blowing down the middle of the street, we stop the car and reach out, like 'Oh this'll look cool if I wear it' – you know, old newspapers, bags. We rob the bag ladies! Beat 'em up. Take their clothes."

And as for the hair: "It was the direction we were going for years," says Nikki, "and we just perfected it. First you got to cut it real jaggedy. And you need this stuff (*a huge bottle of Flex Net pump hairspray*). Then you've got to dry your hair upside down and pull it out while you do it. Of course you've got to sleep upside-down, you sleep on your forehead. When you wake up in the morning your hair is all messed up, and you look in the mirror and you say, 'I look fine'... We're different. That's all, Maybe a bit ahead of our time even. "In five years, maybe every band will look like us."

One month later they're back at the Starwood, on stage this time, making their debut opening for Y&T. The San Francisco band had a sizeable LA following and the place is packed when Mötley hit the stage. "They were really shocked when we first came out onstage," says Vince. "They didn't know what to do. The other band was like a typical heavy metal hippy-type band – no looks, no concept – and when we came out the audience was just going uuhhhh, what is this?"

A second show the same month – at Pookies sandwich shop in Pasadena – attracted a crowd of 12!

"It was a lot of work," says Mick. "Clubs were more than hesitant. Nikki and I worked day in and day out to get a Tuesday or Wednesday night opening for someone at the Whisky *(the small but perfectly-formed and prestigious rock club on Sunset Strip)* and then you'd try going from a Wednesday to a Thursday night or a weekend."

In the beginning Nikki was managing the band; he knew all the club owners in town from having played with London. But in a scene totally dominated by new wave it was tough. "Nobody took us seriously," says Nikki. "They couldn't get past our image and listen to our music. LA's really trend-oriented, so with the whole new wave thing everyone was really just laughing at us. *The LA Weekly* called us 'LA's worst band'." Then Mick introduced them to the man who would become their first manager.

Allan Coffman, one of Mick's friends' brother-in-law, made his money in the construction business. He was attracted by the idea of investing in a rock band, and put up the money for the Crüe to make a single. 'Stick To Your Guns', backed with 'Toast Of The Town', was recorded in Crystal Sound Studios in June '81. A thousand copies were pressed up, and handed out free at gigs. He also decided they should "test the waters outside of LA" and backed their first tour – a handful of gigs in "Anywhere USA. We had kids from 12 and 13 on up to 35 and 40 come down," said Coffman in an interview at the time. "Everybody's curious, so they come down, and then they like us when they hear the music and find out that it's not just a freakshow."

By the end of the year, Mötley Crüe had its own audience. As Nikki put it, "We just kept picking up other people's audiences until we got one of our own." But still the record companies wouldn't touch them. "All the labels were still signing bands like The Knack," says Mick. "But we knew that we could sell records."

So December '81, barely six months after making their debut, the Crüe go into Hit City West Studio to record their debut album. They take the same route as the punks and the New Wave Of British Heavy Metal bands, getting a grassroots following and bypassing the record companies, making a cheap record and putting it out themselves. 'Too Fast For Love' takes three days and $7,000. They release it independently on their own label, Leathür Records.

"We realise," said Coffman at the time, "in all likelihood that the majors are not going to hop on something new and different and radical compared to what's happening now, that they weren't going to be as enthusiastic about it as we are, so from the very beginning we laid out a plan. It was two-fold: working with a major label if they were interested and wanted to work with us, and if that didn't happen then we'd go down the other road which was eventually to build to a point where we establish our own label."

Nikki Sixx: "It's more difficult this way, but in the long run it's going to be better for us and better for the audience. We have control. The reaction of some of the majors has been 'yeah, it's real good but you'll have to change this and change that'. We're not going to change nothing to fit into somebody else's concept who sits in an office on the 17th floor and has never stood in the audience."

At first they press up just 900 copies of the album – a real collector's item, it's got white lettering instead of red and in the band photos on the back Vince has a hilarious beehive toupee perched on top of his shag-do. The second pressing – 15,000 copies in all – has red lettering and Vince looking a bit more sensible. On the front, a close-up of a well-used third of the singer's anatomy, black, laced-crotched leather pants, a gloved hand hovering dangerously near. A rip off from Japan's album sleeve, sure, but they nicked it from the Stones' 'Sticky Fingers'!

The music is ragged, fast and furious. 'Live Wire' – *"Plug me in I'm alive tonight"*, raw and dirty. 'Public Enemy' – *"Climbing high, fast as the speed of sound... don't think about nothin' because we're gonna get crazy"*. 'Stick To Your Guns' – *"Hey man I'm screaming, are you watching me bleed, are you believing?"*. 'Take Me To The Top', 'Piece Of Your Action'. Some classic Crüe songs; trashy, sleazy, hooky, heavy, something American metal hasn't been for a long, long time.

"I walked into Licorice Pizza the other day *(the record store that used to be opposite the Whisky)* and the girl goes they sold all our records out faster than any band ever," said Nikki a week after its release. Both pressings sell right out.

18

Chapter Two
Take Me To The Top

Everyone laughed at me when I brought Mötley Crüe in. Elektra Records was like the home of The Eagles and Jackson Browne and Linda Ronstadt. I said, 'You know what? This fucking record company needs some fucking rock'n'roll!' Because Elektra started with The Stooges and MC5 in the late '60s and it was really a radical, high-energy rock label. And I said, 'We need a little bit less laid-back Southern California thing, because we've got all the best of that music, now let's find something for the kids of the '80s'."

In June 1982, as the Crüe launch their disastrous Canadian tour (they were booked into gay bars and discos) by having their stage props and costumes confiscated by customs as offensive weapons, A&R man Tom Zutaut signs the band to Elektra. In August 'Too Fast For Love' – which has sold out all 20,000 of its original copies and has been given to Queen producer Roy Thomas Baker to tart up – gets a major label release. The Elektra version has bigger printing and smaller band photos and omits the track 'Stick To Your Guns'. ("We had to remove a song to give it more clarity as the less grooves you have on the vinyl," said Nikki, "the louder and clearer it becomes. So it was either 'Stick To Your Guns' or 'One With The Show', and we chose the former.") It sounds less raggedy than the Leathür version too. ("I don't think it has enough nuts... I prefer the original.") But it's still exaggerated, over-the-top and teeming with the kind of songs your mother disapproves of. It enters the US album charts at Number 157.

But things aren't going so good.

"We were depressed," says Vince.

Nikki: "We kind of had to stop and get everything organised around us, because we were so screwed up. We didn't have anything left to pawn even. There was no money at all."

Vince: "At that point we were making $20 a week."

Nikki: "We even had to go out and nick four turkey pies to have a Christmas dinner."

Vince: "We stole a Christmas tree and put beer cans on it for decorations."

Nikki: "And we had to play that day, so we woke up and looked at the Christmas tree, we took it outside and we lit it on fire and left for the gig."

Vince: "It was a really depressing year. It couldn't get any worse. Me and Nikki would go and sit under University Stereo (*a hi-fi shop on the Sunset Strip*), sitting with the bums drinking, we'd buy some cheap wine and some vodka and we'd sit underneath in the alleyway and drink and go, 'We're fairly good-looking guys, the band's all right, so how come we're sitting here on the streets of Hollywood?'."

And only a couple of months ago they were draped across the pages of *Oui*, the men's magazine!

Vince: "That's another manager story. We looked awful, those chicks were awful. He would make all these decisions without even asking us. It's been a bad year."

In December of '82 they play a show at the Santa Monica Civic, the 3500 seater hall down by the ocean that they packed out earlier in the year, inviting just about every manager in town. Among them, Doc McGhee and Doug Thaler. At the time their company, McGhee Entertainment, was involved in local New York concert promotions, slowly building an organisation that could handle management representation for aspiring acts. The Crüe take them on board. A couple of months later – their efforts to stage the First Annual Nude Miss Heavy Metal Contest at the Santa Monica Civic having been thwarted by officials citing bylaws prohibiting the depravity of minors – Mötley are out opening for Kiss on their 'Creatures Of The Night' US tour (Kiss' last in their celebrated make-up) playing to their biggest crowds, 15,000 a night – a warm-up for their appearance in May at the Us Festival.

The Us Festival took place over three days in a huge hot dusty site on the outskirts of LA that looked like someone had turned every vacuum cleaner bag in the world upside down on an orgy. The first day was new music – The Clash, Men At Work and some Woodstocky satellite link with the Soviet Union. The third day featured mainstream rock acts – David Bowie, Missing Persons, The Pretenders. But the second day, heavy metal day, had the biggest attendance by far. Over 300,000 specimens of beer-drinking, leather-clad humanity paid $20 apiece for a bill that would bring tears to your eyes if the smog hadn't already done so: Van Halen, Scorpions, Triumph, Judas Priest, Ozzy Osbourne, Mötley Crüe and Quiet Riot.

Quiet Riot, a bunch of Slade disciples who are also rising stars on the LA glam metal scene, go on first, in the morning. The sun's beating down and the temperature over 100 degrees when Mötley follow on at half past noon. ("I hope gin and tonics work at 12.30," said Nikki beforehand.) The audience sings along with 'Live Wire', Vince's voice croaking in the dust, and there are shouts from the back for an encore – a cover of The Beatles 'Helter Skelter'.

That, and an appearance in October on MTV's *Halloween Horror Show*, are the breakthrough Mötley need. At the Us Festival they played to 300,000 metal fans ready to be won over. On MTV – a live concert shot at the Limelight Club in Chicago – they played to millions.

When Music Television was launched in the States on August 1, 1981, it changed the face of music. MTV ran music videos 24 hours a day, seven days a week. The material it needed was of young, good-looking bands that wouldn't scare the TV viewers away from the pimple cream ads. The stadium bands that dominated the US charts – the Styxs, Journeys, Air Supplys, Loverboys, Foreigners – were either too fat or faceless to attract the demographic MTV was after; permed hair and middle-aged buttocks squeezed into tight jeans is not going to attract the advertisers. So they turned to the British new wave bands, then the prettier of the New Wave Of British Heavy Metal bands, like Def Leppard, and as LA produced its own young, sexy, image-conscious metal bands, they too got saturation play. By 1983, MTV had an estimated 15 million viewers in the 12 to 34 age group. Around a third of the videos on heavy rotation that year are hard rock or heavy metal.

So, when the Crüe's second album, 'Shout At The Devil', comes out in November, the audience is there, waiting for them, dollars at the ready. 'Shout...' sells 200,000 copies in two weeks. (Fellow Us Festival openers and MTV stars Quiet Riot, incidentally, are equally successful with their debut album 'Metal Health'.) It reaches Number 17 in the US charts, eventually selling three million copies.

It's two years since the indie release of 'Too Fast For Love'. It looks like a different lifetime. You get the big money package treatment, the gatefold cover with the expensive black-on-black embossed pentagram to lure you in, and the four sleaze gods inside dressed and made up like expensive whores, reeking of record company investment. Happily, underneath the futuristic outfits and the professional hairdos and the pancake and blusher and lipstick carefully applied like some upwardly-mobile secretary, it's still the same bad-living, offensive, gloriously unacceptable Mötleys – just given a wash and brush-up for public consumption. The man given the job of cleaning them up this time is Tom Werman, a corporate rock style producer who has worked with Ted Nugent and Cheap Trick.

The song 'Bastard' holds a special place in the band's heart. It's written about and dedicated to their former manager, Allan Coffman, whom they accuse of absconding with their money and thus holding up the recording of their second LP. *"Out go the lights/In goes my knife... consider that bastard dead/Get on your knees... you're the king of the sleaze."*

The hot and sweaty 'Ten Seconds To Love' is "dedicated to the beer bottle twins," says Vince, in a none too subtle reference to their notorious backstage shenanigans. *"Bring a girlfriend, maybe bring two... Let's inject it/Photograph it."* They certainly did photograph it. During their stint on the road with Ozzy, his wife and manager Sharon Osbourne confiscated the Crüe's backstage passes and banned them from bringing playmates backstage after she caught them taking polaroids of a line-up of groupies in very compromising positions! 'Knock 'Em Dead Kid' smoulders. *"Heard a steel-belted scream... Another sidewalk's bloody dream/My blood turned to freeze/You'll see the red in my eyes as you take my disease."* So does 'Looks That Kill' – "a song with a double meaning," according to Nikki. "A beautiful woman or a woman killer."

And of course there's 'Shout At The Devil', just made for arena punch-alongs. But the Devil? And Pentagrams?

Blackie Lawless of WASP: "Nikki came to me and he goes, 'Are you going to use the pentagram? Will you teach me to set myself on fire?' and all that stuff that he did. He said. 'Are you going to use any of that stuff any more?'. I said no. He says, 'Would you mind if I use it?'. I said, you can take whatever you like, but before you do so I must warn you that you're tampering with something that you do not know what you're dealing with. Magic, be it black or white, is a bad influence. Because it will cause you to do things in your life that you don't want to do. I've never known a band that ever got into it, or people in general, that did not have serious tragedy befall them time after time. I don't have to go into detail."

In the light of the following year's events, it makes you stop and think. However, the Crüe have a different outlook on it when Sylvie talks to them for *Sounds* in October '83.

Nikki: "Shout at the Devil. Not with him. We're as anti-Satan as a band can get. We're not like into being Christians or Catholics, but the Devil has nothing to do with Mötley Crüe... We've studied it – like I read up on this book called *The Necronomacon*. There was so much of that going around and I didn't know what it was about."

Vince: "We don't sacrifice goats or anything like that."

Nikki: "We sacrifice little 13 year old girls though! We're saying shout at the devil – your teachers, police, politicians, anybody that's an authoritative figure that puts you down or doesn't let you achieve what you want to do in life. Shout at the motherfucker! Do what you want to do! That's what 'Shout At The Devil' is about. The pentagram has nothing to do with Satan. It's the symbol of the werewolf."

Vince: "It wards off werewolves. If you wear a pentagram and there's a werewolf around he won't fuck with you."

Nikki: "It's a very positive symbol. Our mascot's the werewolf."

Vince: "We're contradicting ourselves."

Nikki: "Okay, a kind of a werewolf."

Vince: "A Mötley Wölf! He kind of looks like us – on bad nights. He's got part black hair, part white hair."

Nikki: "We used the pentagram because we like to get into any trouble we can. What's the worst symbol you can find, short of a swastika? All this heavy metal devil worship shit that's going around – we're just us, we're the same band we've always been. I don't even think we're heavy metal – we're just a rock'n'roll band. We've got catchy melodies on top. We haven't changed."
Their image has, though, judging by the 'Shout...' sleeve.

"People look at the 'Too Fast For Love' album cover and then look at 'Shout At The Devil' and they say, 'Oh, it looks so drastically different'. First of all," says Nikki, "the pictures on 'Too Fast...' are black and white, we've got red lipstick on and the white on our face, but you can't see it because it's black and white. And it's slowly evolved. We couldn't afford costumes like that before. I couldn't afford a cool outfit so I wore duct tape on my arm and wrapped myself up in a telephone cord. Basically we were as outrageous as we are now two years ago, because nobody looked like us or dressed like us onstage. All these bands started copying us, dressing like us, dyeing their hair black or white. We had to keep one step ahead of everybody."

The first time we spoke to them, Mötley claimed that in five years' time every band would look like them. It's actually happened in half the time. LA is teeming with Mötley look-alike bands, flyposters advertising club gigs by dozens of bands with two XXs in their names yellowing in the hot sun.

"It's ridiculous," says Vince. "You can't tell one from the other. I'll go down the Troubadour and I'll see a band up there and I'll go, 'Hey, didn't I see you guys the other night?' They all look the same, and they all sound the same."

Heavy metal – LA metal – has caught on like a forest fire. The record companies who ignored metal in favour of new wave little more than a year ago are haunting the streets of Hollywood, sniffing the air for hairspray and leather and falling at the feet of anything with big hair, lipstick and a guitar, to offer up their chequebooks.

24

Tom Zutaut, the man who signed Mötley: "If you're in LA right now *(1983)* and you're not playing heavy metal and you're playing synthesiser drone music, then you're in trouble. The record companies are looking at these millions of records sold and flipping out. They're saying, 'Where's our Def Leppard? Where's our Quiet Riot? Why the fuck are we promoting Duran Duran?'."

Los Angeles, a place more associated with laid-back Southern California soft rock and Smiley bumper stickers, has taken over as the headbanging capital of the world. When Chris Stein, guitarist with leading New York new wave band Blondie, popped West he moaned, "For God's sake, is that all you people in LA want to hear? Aggressive lyrics and a raging guitar?". As any true metal fan would answer: what other kind of lyrics are there? What other kind of guitar? An article in the American tabloid *The Weekly World News* at the end of the year reflects what any rock fan already knows. Heavy metal is suddenly happening. It's everywhere.

"Loony teens bash their brains out in sicko dance craze. Like jungle beasts gone bonkers, our freaked-out teens are bashing their brains out in a sick new dance fad called headbanging. And now this mania is sweeping the States, leaving dozens of teenagers dead or maimed forever!"

Chapter Three – God Bless The Children Of The Beast

A day in the life . . .

Nikki: "I sleep till three or four in the afternoon. It takes a few hours to get drunk, then back on the street again."

Vince: "Pass out, wake up, go back out."

Nikki: "We started drinking at five in the afternoon one day – we had this big bottle of Jack Daniel's, finished that off and went to get another one. We waited for the Whisky to open – we lived above the Whisky (*up the hill from the club, to be precise*) and we stumbled out of there right as the doors opened, eight o'clock."

Vince: "We were wasted."

Nikki: "And I can't find Vince, and there's only two people in the club! I found him underneath the car outside. He was passed out, sleeping. I had to carry him home. Just imagine. Me. Carrying this guy!"

Vince: "With his high heels on up this steep hill. I woke up a couple of hours later, about eleven. 'Okay, let's party!'."

Nikki: "Went out and got drunk again. Seriously fucked-up."

Vince: "It said on our baby bottles: 'serious fuck-up'. We've been like this from day one. At school I'd always sit at the back so I could take drugs. I had this pipe that looked like a pen and no smoke ever came out of it... I don't condone kids using drugs. I just condone them for myself and for the band. We're old enough to know how to use it."

Nikki: "I figure you only go around once and nobody gets out alive, so live it to its fullest. I wouldn't say everybody should live life like that. We're like a rare breed, like the kids on the block that they warned you about type of thing." "Every mother's nightmare," Vince grins. "That's what we are."

And every young girl's dream. Their audience now is divided roughly 50/50 along gender lines. (MTV takes the credit for helping metal cross over from its predominantly male audience, but the Crüe had a loyal female following from the outset.) And the audience is huge. As 1984 rolls around, they have two albums in the US charts, as the success of 'Shout...' shoves 'Too Fast...' into the Billboard Top 100 – and licence to go completely over the top.

"We were always rowdy," says Nikki, and he's telling the truth. "We're not faking, we're just us. We drink and fuck and do drugs – doesn't everybody? The only difference now is we can afford better drugs! People are going, 'Nikki, I've never seen you smile so much'. I'm happier now than I've ever been in my whole life.

"I didn't expect it to happen so quickly, but it feels good. It feels good to walk into your record company offices and everybody's opening their doors and smiling and all the secretaries are going, 'Hi Nikki, how are you?' all friendly, when it wasn't all that long ago that they used to ignore us or run away screaming. We're having fun," Nikki beams. "Jesus, we're having fun."

Ask any rock'n'roll musician why they first got into rock and they won't say to save the rainforests, to see the world, to meet studio engineers or play two major chords, a minor and a diminished seventh. No, ten times out of ten they'll tell you they got into rock to get laid (and if they don't, they're either in a politically correct alternative band or they're lying). When Nikki, Tommy, Mick and Vince are handed the fruits of success, they bite on them like starving men. Literally. Tales start circulating about groupies leaving the backstage area covered with teethmarks. At a party in Europe, Nikki and Tommy descend on David Lee Roth, teeth bared, and bite him too. Along with drawing genitals on walls and crowds to concerts, Mötley Crüe like to draw blood!

"We bite the fuck out of people who come on the bus with us," laughs Nikki. Mötley have a bus rule: all women who get on board have to go topless; if you want to go to the back you take the lot off; the stuff involving bottles and the rest we won't touch with bargepoles. What some people will do to meet stars is and always has been incredible. Anyway. "We bite the fuck out of each other too. Tommy bites me and I bite him all the time. We bite our audiences too – all the time! We get paid in flesh. Our audiences," he declares with affection, "are sluts."

Their tour with Ozzy Osbourne at the start of '84 is every bit as crazy as you'd expect: thrown out of Germany for tossing double beds out of hotel windows and watching them bounce off of car roofs, so many groupies backstage that even the tolerant Sharon Osbourne (Mrs Ozzy) objects. The band ask Ozzy photographer Ross 'The Master' Halfin onto the bus to take photographs of them being serviced in the lap department by assorted naked females – there's talk of getting the blow-job pictures printed in *Hustler* magazine. The Crüe photo album is already starting to rival the infamous Kiss one. Says *Rolling Stone*: "they're almost the Sex Pistols of heavy metal."

In August 1984, they finally make it to Britain – to play the Castle Donington Festival. Mötley are at the bottom of the bill, AC/DC at the top, and in between Accept, Y&T (the Crüe's first-ever gig was opening for this Bay Area band) Gary Moore, Ozzy Osbourne and fellow Los Angelenos Van Halen.

Tommy: "I was so fucking excited! I'd heard and read so much about the Donington festival that I was shitting myself waiting to go over and play. And at the same time I was real scared, because I heard about how the English fans, if they don't like you, pelt the fuck out of you with whatever they can get their hands on – bottles of piss, whatever. Just before the end of our set I looked down at the stage and there was hardly any shit on there. I thought, 'Fuck! They like us'!"

They do. The crowd is still pouring in as the Crüe come on at noon – half an hour before their Us Festival performance, half an hour before their scheduled performance time for some reason. The sun, amazingly for Donington, is blazing mercilessly. The band are shoehorned into multi-coloured leather. They launch their set with a scorching 'Bastard'. The half-hearted missile-throwing that traditionally greets the opening act soon stops. By the end of the set – which includes 'Ten Seconds To Love', 'Looks That Kill' and 'Live Wire' – "victory," according to *Kerrang!*'s live review, "had been secured. The Crüe proved conclusively to the British headbanging public that their success Stateside hasn't been built on image alone. The band rip out real metal thunder, tighter and heavier than any other LA act you care to mention. The likes of Quiet Riot," Derek Oliver writes, "are simply laughable in comparison."
They end the set with 'Helter Skelter'. A fan is injured when Nikki smashes his bass guitar and throws it from the stage. Then again, something pretty weird was thrown at Mötley...

Tommy: "You know what they threw at us? An eyeball! I swear to God. It was oozing with stuff. Someone threw it onstage and it got wedged in my drum riser. My drum tech comes back to me after the show and he grabs me and goes, 'Tommy, you've got to fucking see this. I've never seen anything like it in my life'. I went out to my drums as they're loading them away and there's this fucking eyeball. It looks like it could have come from a cow or a horse or something – it was a lot larger than a human eyeball. It was so fucking hideous! Where did that come from?"

Well, someone smuggled a pig's head into Donington and threw it at Bon Jovi. Could this be the solution to the mystery?

"Maybe Jonny got a pig that had one eye!" Tommy laughs. "No-one has ever thrown a fucking eyeball at us. I was so shocked!"

There's a story that the band had to negotiate with the festival's promoters over the number of times they could say 'fuck' from the Donington stage.

Apparently they compromised on 21.

Tommy again: "We always get these fucking promoters who say, 'Well you're in this city tonight and it's a big no-no to say fuck' – so obviously the first thing

30

Vince does, he says fuck in the first song like four hundred fucking times, just to piss everybody off. That's probably where that story stems from – it happens all the time. We never negotiated."

Mötley follow-up this appearance at Donington by accepting an offer to support top British metal act Iron Maiden in Europe. Prior to this series of dates, Maiden host a special party in London, to which the Mötley boys are duly invited. The press, representatives of Maiden's record company (EMI) and management (Smallwood-Taylor), as well as various rock'n'roll luminaries are all in attendance. But that matters little to the LA wild boys.

On the prowl for drugs – anything stimulatory – they descend on *Kerrang!* journalist Xavier Russell. Despite the hapless scribe's protestations that, no, he doesn't have any drugs on him, the band insist on checking for themselves, in the process lifting him bodily off the floor and turning him upside down. Loose change that Xavier had forgotten to glue to his pockets falls like a rain of silver – but, no, he hasn't any drugs.

However, if Mötley create some degree of havoc at the shindig, that's nothing to the practical joke perpetrated on them by aforementioned photographer Ross Halfin. Having in his possession the infamous photos taken earlier in the year on the Mötley tour bus (*Hustler* aren't interested in using them), Ross decides to get one particular shot blown up of Tommy being... er, blown up as it were by an especially accommodating young lady. Having had it made into a poster, Ross then gives the offending item to his mother, Enid and Connie Collen, mother of Def Leppard guitarist Phil. Their instructions are to take this poster over to Tommy at the party and ask him, in all innocence, to autograph it.

Thus, the die is cast. Enid and Connie (two harmless-looking middle-aged women) wander over to Tommy at a given signal and present him with the poster (rolled up) for his signature. Tommy, feeling mighty happy that he is being asked for his autograph, smiles and unrolls the poster – only to be presented with a sight that takes his breath away! Almost lost for words, Tommy asks the two women confronting him where they obtained the poster, to which Ross' mother replies, "Oh, we bought it from a trader outside the Hammersmith Odeon" (where Maiden had played that night).
For a split second, Tommy is stunned. But then he catches Ross' eye – and realises he's being duped. Whether Tommy ever forgave Master Halfin for this wind-up is open to conjecture!

By the time they leave for the European leg of the Iron Maiden 'Powerslave' tour, the Crüe are totally fired up. So much so that when they hit France, one of their hotel rooms goes up in flames! Possibly spontaneous combustion, though probably more to do with the fact that the band were playing with flare guns at the time. Mötley have been serious pyromaniacs (as well as other sort of maniacs) since day one. Blackie Lawless, Nikki's colleague in London, takes credit for getting him to play with fire.

It is true that when they both left the three-year-old LA band – Nikki to work with Tommy Lee, Blackie to form WASP – they both made pyro a big part of their shows. In the early days, Nikki talked a lot about theatrical rock and seemed to want the same level of theatre in the Crüe's stage show as WASP had in theirs. In an interview in 1982 as 'Too Fast For Love' came out, Nikki talked about finally making the kind of money to put on the kind of show he wanted: "more on a Broadway-type level. Or old Tubes or Alice Cooper stuff. I mean, after Kiss made 20 foot high flames eight feet around, you can't top that with a little smokebomb. Theatrical, yeah, but on a real theatre level. Our next album (*which, remember, will be 'Shout At The Devil'*) is going to be very concept-oriented so the whole thing can be acted out onstage, and we'll build up from that album on. Basically it's a TV and violence type concept and we're going to break that into a show using us as characters and other people as characters within the whole concept. Our show's going to be like a movie. We have some songs written." What happened to them, Mötley alone know. But the concept album and show idea is something Nikki doesn't drop. He's still talking about it this year. Maybe their third album, 'Theatre Of Pain', will exorcise the theatre obsession a little.

But fire's not so easy to put out. Their show features 32 smoke bombs, Vince's flaming sword, Tommy's flaming drum sticks, and Nikki wears thigh-high boots that Vince sets alight – or when they're headlining, anyway.
Nikki: "When we're opening for other bands they aren't exactly thrilled with the idea. I mean imagine going up to Def Leppard and saying 'Mind if I set the bass player on fire?'. It's kind of hard to top that with jeans and tennis shoes and going out and singing 'Photograph'."

Vince: "When we first started to perfect setting him on fire, we used to practice in our apartment."

Nikki: "And the alarm's going off and the manager walks into the building."

Vince: "And we'd just got these smoke bombs for onstage and we're trying to see how much smoke they made. We lit them off, all these different colours inside our apartment, and it's staining the ceiling red and blue."

Nikki: "Needless to say, they asked us to move out."

They're not much safer in the outside world. Nikki got arrested once for setting fire to a palm tree...

November '84. No palm trees in London, just endless cold, pissing rain. After Crüe leave the Maiden tour they play their first UK headlining gig at the Dominion Theatre. The now-forgotten Stratus (featuring ex-Maiden drummer Clive Burr and not much else) are the opening act – limp pomp rock. Mötley Crüe couldn't have been more opposite: sleazy, hooky, confident, heavy, sexy, flash (as if to prove the latter, Tommy Lee moons the crowd with his Blackie Lawless-style bottomless leather pants!).

There's a futuristic, *Escape From New York*-style stage set, blinding lights at the foot of the drum platform, dry ice, flashbins, fireworks and brilliant music. It starts mean and nasty with 'Bastard' – sung, like every other number, like a grand finale. Halfway through there's a brand new song – the Dominion audience is the first on the planet to hear it – the anthemic 'Raise Your Hands To Rock'. (It will appear on their 1985 album 'Theatre Of Pain'.) Then the classics keep coming: 'A Piece Of My Action', 'Looks That Kill', 'Live Wire' and closer 'Helter Skelter'. There's an ambulance outside the theatre. Probably handing out tranquillisers, judging by the crazed crowd reaction.

Back to LA for a short break before starting work on the new album. Nikki has already started writing songs. Vince is partying. Razzle, drummer with wasted Finn glam metal legends Hanoi Rocks, is hanging with a bunch of people at Vince's house at Redondo Beach, a half hour or so drive from LA. They run out of booze. Vince, Razzle and a couple of thirsty visitors pile into the Crüe frontman's flash Ford Pantera to go to the liquor store down the road. The car skids, Vince loses control. He smashes into an oncoming Volkswagen. The driver and passenger in the VW are injured.

Razzle is dead.

HANOI ROCKS — Drummer, Razzle on left

together some of the biggest names in metal – but we'll come to that later. For the moment, though, whilst the world is beginning to wake up to the confirmation of contemporary music's potent clout and its ability to change the world (the Band Aid single 'Do They Know It's Christmas?', released at the end of 1984, had already put the plight of the famine victims on the map and set the ball rolling with an irresistible momentum), Mötley Crüe are more concerned with what's going on close to home. The band are about to face the first real crisis of their colourful career: the accident, or more to the point, its repercussions.

There have been other accidents, sure: Nikki totalled his Corvette driving home legless (and, stranger still, clothesless!) from the Rainbow Bar And Grill. Did the same thing with his second Corvette – but all he had to show for it was a smashed collarbone and a scar where he dislocated his shoulder. Tommy was doing 90 on the freeway (the US speed limit, as any Sammy Hagar fan would know, is 55 mph) out of his gourd when he lost control, went off the road, the car rolling over. Vince managed to smash a yacht on a cruise out to Catalina Island, just off LA, last year. But this accident, this was different. Someone's dead. You can't just put a pin in your arm or a new wing on the car or an Alka Seltzer in a glass of water and make things right. The Law is involved.

Following the tragic death of Razzle, it seems inevitable that Vince will be charged with something, possibly vehicular manslaughter, and in January '85, this prophecy is duly fulfilled. Under his full name of Vince Neil Wharton, the

singer is summarily charged with the offence and released on $2,500 bail. Now, most people expect that this will inevitably lead to a lengthy prison term for Vince, that the authorities will go out of their way to make an exhibition of this 'depraved rock star'. Vince seems to go along with this way of thinking as well, as he turns up at the courtroom in a sober suit with his first wife (from whom he's rumoured to be estranged) respectably by his side. Veritable theses are written by so-called 'experts' on whether or not the blond vocalist could survive a term in jail, and there are those who gleefully predict that the wheels are about to come off the tearaway Mötley bandwagon.

The band were out of control, went one theory. Could Razzle's death signify the end for the Mötleys? Others felt that this incident might shock them out of their parabolically decadent state and straighten them out. Whatever, most waited for the law to take a firm stance – and then we'd see what the next move would be. It looked like Blackie Lawless's pentagram prediction was coming true: "I've never known a band that ever got into *(black magic)* that did not have serious tragedy befall them..."

However, much to everyone's surprise, when Neil is finally brought to trial and found guilty, the court's judgement is astonishingly lenient. He's sentenced to spend 30 days in jail, undertake 200 hours of community service and pay $2.6 million to Razzle's family and the two people injured – namely Louis Smithers and Lisa Hogan – in the other car. To say that shockwaves went through the rock world is to put it mildly. It seemed that some form of deal had been struck out of court between all the parties concerned, and that angered some who felt that Neil had been let off incredibly lightly because of who he was and the huge financial backing to which he had ready access. It was being claimed in some quarters that justice had neither been done nor been seen to be done.

Most vociferous in their condemnation are certain journalists who knew Hanoi Rocks and felt as if Razzle's death had been too easily dismissed by the Mötley camp as nothing more than an irritant. Hanoi's career was over. The Finnish glam giants split up shortly afterwards, unable to come to terms with the loss of their drummer. And that merely added fuel to the fire.

There were even some Hanoi fans who went so far as to suggest that there should be picket lines outside venues wherever Mötley played. Needless to say, this never happened and the protests slowly subsided. But looking at the situation in the cold light of day a decade on, it is easier to view dispassionately the entire sorry saga and to feel that a long jail term for Neil (in the end he was only to spend 20 days in jail anyway at the conclusion of the 'Theatre Of Pain' tour) would have served no real purpose.

What has to be borne in mind is that this was an accident: that part of the reason Vince's powerful vehicle careered out of control was because of the state of the road, and that Razzle himself was quite aware of the inebriated state Vince was in when he got into the car.

None of this excuses the singer in the slightest, but it does perhaps make it a little easier to understand just why the final verdict was not as tough as it might have been.

In addition, the whole band voluntarily undertake to give anti drink-driving lectures at schools and colleges throughout America. They also donate $17,500 to an anti drink-driving organisation in the States.

"We didn't have to do it," Nikki tells Sylvie. "We don't have to do anything. See, the funny thing about that accident is – it's kind of ironic. Tommy got in a really bad car accident, 90mph, rolled over nine times off the freeway, he was fucked-up really bad. I smashed a Porsche into a telephone pole and did this," he shows his shoulder scar, "and I was really drunk. And Vince, who was barely drunk, just barely, going up the street, there's a wet spot with moss growing on the water and he's got a powerful car, a Pantera, he's giving it a bit of gas and the car hits it and someone dies. And Vince is just barely drunk – nothing like me or Tommy. But no-one died in our cars. We just said, there are four people in the band, three people have fucked up bad, one person's dead, one person's got a shattered shoulder, another person has a fucking maimed hand from other accidents – and two days before my accident I almost killed somebody opening the door, ripped the door off the car. And I said, do you know what? I love to drink. I love to be fucked-up. But I'm not going to drive any more. I think we should tell our fans, don't drink and drive. Not don't drink – do whatever you want to do man, shoot up heroin, I don't care, have fun, it's your life, but don't get in a car when you do it, because it's metal and we have skin, and with skin and metal, the metal wins. That's all we're saying. People go, 'Oh Mötley Crüe are mellowing out'. And I go, well if all that means is we care about our fans then fuck you, man!"

Yet, there were also those who felt that Mötley's stock had, if anything, risen because of this whole sad affair. It proved that here was a band prepared to go to the edge – and leap. They seemed to know no bounds and were simply staring down fate. People always have a morbid fascination, an attraction if you like, with those who've experienced death at close hand. Neil had been responsible for another's demise – the ultimate expression of power (or some such nonsense). This added a certain lustre to Mötley's image. Unsavoury, unhealthy it might have been, but this is a fact of life. No harm had really been done to their reputation.

Furthermore, there seems no end in sight to the wild lifestyle the band are leading. They're as crazy and stimulant-driven as ever, if not more so. The money was now available to fuel such indulgences at a new level of obsession, the lesson of the car crash having been ingested and then seemingly vomited straight back out. The band are still partying as if tomorrow would never dawn – as if, in certain cases, they hoped tomorrow would never dawn?

39

40

When Sylvie goes to Germany to interview the band, Vince's sentence is hanging over their head. Vince is sober – sitting around backstage drinking cokes. Nikki's getting through a hell of a lot of coke himself, but it doesn't come in bottles!

The band's British record company office asks Sylvie to bring back Nikki's stage costume with her – they want to give it out as a competition prize. Stopped by Customs at Heathrow Airport, they pull the crumpled stage outfit out of her bag and hold it up to look at it. Bundled into her bag as soon as Nikki took it off, it still bears the marks of last night's festivities: a shower of thin white dust sprinkles off it onto the ground. "Baby powder," says Sylvie innocently, as visions of a holiday in Holloway Prison dance before her eyes.
Before she left Germany she asked Nikki, when the tour is over does Vince have to go to jail? Nikki sobers up for a moment. "Yeah." And has the band made plans to deal with it, or are they kind of acting like it's not really happening? Again a hesitant reply.

"Vince, uh, has gone through a lot. He's had to pay a lot of money. He's learnt to live with – uh – the death. And we as a band were very good friends with Hanoi Rocks, and I'm still very good friends with Andy McCoy and Mike Monroe. So – uh – it saddens me. Vince, he's a grown man, he can take care of it. And I'm going to go straight home to start working on the next album because that's my thing, that's my love in life, music. So – he does his thing and everyone will stay away from each other for maybe a month or so, and then we'll get together and start working on the next record."

Back on the musical trail, Mötley begin work with producer Tom Werman on their next album in April 1985. It is a crucial record in many respects. The band had achieved so much success with the triple platinum 'Shout At The Devil' – not the least being the huge influence they now wielded over a new generation of aspiring rock stars – that many were wondering if they could really follow it up with something equally as devastating. Moreover, one wondered how the death of Razzle would affect the musical direction and lyrical touch. And would that court case hurt the Mötley sales base – or even improve it?

Work on the record is relatively quick and efficient. Titled 'Theatre Of Pain' (now there was a box of demons wrapped up in three words! Was this phrase a cynical insight into the band's psychological profile?), the album is duly released in June. It includes the following dedication on the sleeve: "This album is dedicated to Nicholas 'Razzle' Dingley". There is also a message to Crüe fans: "If and/or when you drink – Don't take the wheel. Live and learn – so we can all fuckin' rock our ass off together for a long time to come."

Masks of comedy and tragedy adorn the sleeve, aptly mirroring the circumstances under which it was written. A bit of an interlude album, this one – not surprising considering its chronological position (third albums are

47

48

Chapter five – Home Sweet Home

"This is a song about being on the road, which we call 'Home Sweet Home'..." Home sweet home smells of beer and cigarettes and things they advertise in the sticky back pages of *Penthouse*. Home sweet home – the Mötley tour bus – is right now parked outside a grim hall on a grim street in a grim city in Germany.

The hall, long and narrow, looks like an aircraft hangar. Half the American airforce is in there anyway, lots of bare necks and scrubbed ears and off-duty leather, going ape.

"Then – more screams. A horde of teens lunged towards four young men entering the inn, a scene recalling the bygone days of Beatlemania, except this time it was called Mötley-mania", went a report in the American Forces In Germany newspaper *Stripes*.

January '86. The Crüe are on their first headlining tour of Europe following sold-out dates in the States and Japan. It's a scaled-down show from the celebrated one they took around America; the props just physically won't fit into the European venues. Still they do manage to fit in Tommy Lee's spectacular revolving drum set (it shunts forward during the drummer's solo in 'Louder Than Hell', then tips upside down, leaving him hanging and hammering like a bat locked out of Hades). But only just. The ceiling's so low he singes his hair on the overhead lights tonight when the drums turn back the right way up.

And of course there's lots of pyro. Nikki doesn't set himself on fire any more. Just accidentally, now and then. At an outdoor show in Alpine Valley, the pyro went off at the wrong time and literally knocked Vince, Mick and Nikki off their feet.

"I was wearing these sunglasses," says Nikki, "and if I hadn't had them I'd be like Johnny Winter, I'd be blind. Johnny Winter's not blind? Okay, like Stevie Wonder then!

"I saw Johnny Winter last night. He's got some cool tattoos. I love tattoos," muses the bass player, whose body is becoming more and more etched by the month. "I'm addicted. I want to have them everywhere. Well, I guess I have got them everywhere," he grins, revealing a pair of tattooed red lips in a very intimate place... No girl's name carved on his skin, then?

"I have a hard time ever having a girlfriend, because I'm a tramp! I tried. I had a girl, but she got bored with me or I got bored with her."

49

"So now," he laughs, "Robbin's back at my house!" – Robbin Crosby of Ratt and Nikki used to live together in the Crüe's early days, hang out together, go to gigs together, get into fights together. Nikki would walk into a 7-11 store, start a fight, and the large guitarist would step in to save him getting slaughtered. Then, having taken their evening's exercise, they'd go down to whatever club had a cool band playing and empty the bar. The good old days?

"Yeah... We can't do that as much as we used to. It's sad, because it's more self-destructive now," he says revealingly. "Because now we can afford to buy pounds of this drug and pounds of that drug and fucking bottles and bottles of this, and just sit in our house – I bought myself a house with a recording studio, and I just sit there and get high and write music and whatever's inside of me comes out. And if you think about it, that's bad. Because I never go out of the house. I never get to see any of the world outside.

"I've been writing songs for the next album – I've got about seven." A concept album, he says. "Basically it's to do with subliminal messages in television commercials. Like how it says 'Buy Bacardi' and shows them pouring the rum over the ice, and the ice if you really look at it is shaped like a naked woman... So we're going to work off that, but the sex and violence end," says Nikki – echoing what he said in 1982 about the upcoming album, 'Shout At The Devil'. It similarly fails to appear on the band's fourth album, 'Girls, Girls, Girls'.

With 'Home Sweet Home' – released as a double A-side single with 'Smokin' In The Boys' Room' – nudging the UK Top 50, the Mötleys play a nine-date tour of Britain with Cheap Trick as special guests. Paul Henderson reviews it for *Kerrang!*.

"Like gods looking down on their subjects, Mötley Crüe appear atop massive risers, smoke swirling around their feet, lighting trusses dipping and weaving within inches of their heads. The first bomb goes off... 'Looks That Kill', accompanied by suitably thrilling, over-the-top pyrotechnics and explosives... With some degree of justification, the fans go absolutely mental."

And in March, their world tour over, they fly back to LA, home sweet home: Nikki to go to his studio, Vince to go to jail. And Tommy to go down the aisle. On May 10th in Santa Barbara, California, Tommy Lee marries actress Heather Locklear, the beautiful blonde star of the hit TV series *Dynasty*. "That's impressive!" beams the drummer, looking pretty impressive himself in a white leather tuxedo, "this scrawny little tattooed rocker married to this gorgeous fucking girl." He met her at an REO Speedwagon concert – went up to her, took her by the hand and said, 'Hi, I'm Tommy, nice to touch you'. He got her phone number – no honestly, this is true! – from his accountant's brother, who was a dentist who knew Heather's dentist. It's what you call 'networking'. He calls her up. Tells her he's watching her right now on Channel Two.

She turns on her TV and points out it's another actress called Heather he's watching, Heather Thomas. Unfazed, the drummer asks her on a date. It's love. He has her name tattooed on his arm.

Nikki Sixx is best man at the wedding. Guests include members of Ratt, Quiet Riot, Night Ranger and Autograph, Mötley producers Roy Thomas Baker and Tom Werman, and the rest of the Crüe. Even Vince, who has a few more weeks of freedom before doing time.

On June 15th, Vince Neil enters prison. With a third of his sentence commuted for good behaviour, he serves 20 days behind bars.

Meanwhile, in the outside world, it's now been a year since Bob Geldof earned his knighthood and sainthood and whatever other hood they stuck on his stubbled Irish head by organising Live Aid, and thereby achieving the impossible: making pop stars, rock musicians, people whose very existence in an egotistic, cut-throat business means they've only ever seen the world in terms of their glorious selves, feel responsible for a bunch of starving people in a country so far away that they don't even buy their records. In the summer of '86, former Rainbow and Black Sabbath vocalist Ronnie James Dio organises heavy metal's contribution to Ethiopian famine relief: Hear'N'Aid.

Among the cast of thousands on the Band Aid-style single 'Stars' are Ted Nugent, Yngwie Malmsteen, Rob Halford of Judas Priest, Neal Schon of Journey, Kevin Du Brow of Quiet Riot, members of WASP, Queensrÿche, Dio, Iron Maiden and Spinal Tap, and Mick Mars and Vince Neil of Mötley Crüe. Vince is quoted on the Hear'N'Aid video. "If I had a party in my back yard, this is who I'd invite."

By October 1986, the Crüe are back in the studio working on their next album. It should have been ready for release by January 1987, but as things turn out the recording process is to be a little longer than at first conceived.

Talking to *Kerrang!*'s Steffan Chirazi near Christmas '86, Nikki said: "The schedule should see us finished by Christmas and we're looking for a late January release... This album is back nearer the basics of Mötley Crüe music. It's gonna be a raunchy, rocky Crüe classic."

In the end, studio work in LA doesn't finish until February, with the album (by now titled 'Girls, Girls, Girls') eventually put out in May.

Just after the record is completed, Malcolm Dome is granted an impromptu preview whilst in New York. It's a strange tale. Dome was in the Big Apple working on an assignment for *Kerrang!*. One night, he's invited to go and see The Pretenders playing at the Radio City Music Hall by Julie Foley, who worked for McGhee Enterprises (by the way, the hapless Dome managed to fall

asleep at the gig; more a reflection of his state of health than of the performance itself...). Afterwards, Julie suggested they should stop off at the Parker Meridian Hotel in the heart of Manhattan, where Tommy and Nikki were holed up while the album was being mastered. What was meant to be no more than a brief exchange of pleasantries turns into an all-night party!

Tommy and Nikki haul Malcolm, Julie and sundry others, up to the drummer's hotel room, where they're eventually joined by producer Werman and his then-engineer Duane Baron.

Werman has a cassette of the unmastered 'Girls...' album with him, and at Tommy's insistence clamps a set of headphones on Dome and cranks the record out at full volume through a Walkman. With the Mötley duo, plus the production team, intensely watching his every twitch, Dome, a constantly refilling champagne glass in hand, is given the full-on blast of the opus. Superb – and it wasn't just the alcohol talking! One play is enough to convince him that Mötley had come of age and moved into a new dimension.

"Hey, dude, what's your favourite track?" yells Tommy after the tape has wound its course and entered the pit lane. "What d'ya think of the drumming?" Typical drummer, eh? Questions, questions. All of which Dome diplomatically sidesteps. One listen simply isn't sufficient for an informed critique.

The night itself, though, is to provide a slightly worrying insight into the state of health, both mentally and physically, of the Mötley pair. Two of the entourage in that hotel room seem only to be there because they had ready access to drugs in the city. Nikki, in particular, seems anxious for a particular deal to be struck, and when it's agreed over the phone in slightly convoluted language, one of the bassist's bodyguards is despatched to go and cement the deal downtown. When the man returns to the room and gives Nikki the thumbs up, the latter quickly disappears to his own room, returning in a somewhat agitated state. (He is to disappear again a couple of hours later – only that time he doesn't return.) Upon his return Nikki seems especially preoccupied with the rather tawdry state of fellow Los Angeles platinum rockers Ratt, featuring his close friend and erstwhile flat-mate Robbin Crosby. Nikki feels that Ratt needs Werman's production skills to resurrect a failing career.

What starts off as a general discussion between Werman, Sixx, Dome and Baron ends with the Crüe man virtually in hysterics trying to convince the producer that he simply has to agree to contact Ratt and work out a deal. It seems almost as if Nikki had become obsessed by the notion, and it certainly puts a temporary blight on the bonhomie. It is obvious that all is not right with Nikki; subsequent revelations about his heroin addiction lead Dome to presume that he was indeed shooting up that very night, hence his unbalanced viewpoints. What was worrying was that certain members of this entourage had clearly seen it all before, yet were powerless to prevent these excesses.

54

55

Nikki was checked into a drugs rehabilitation clinic during the making of the 'Girls...' album. After ten days he checked out.

"I packed my things," he tells Sylvie, "and hitch-hiked home. I escaped! There were nurses running down the street after me. Really stupid. I threw a typical temper tantrum: 'I don't need this shit! I've been clean for ten days, I can do it on my own!'. It was pretty difficult, because I'm a private person and I'm shy and I just don't want to open up to people that I don't know, so I was really stubborn. I remember this. Everyone's sitting in a circle, they're going on about this and that, 'and now we're going to talk about God'. And I'm pissed off, man I'm pissed off! And they go 'God will do this for you, God will do that for you', and I go, 'FUCK GOD! I'm fucking out of here!'. They're like, 'It's Satan!'. There's this 14-year-old kid there who's been smoking pot going, 'Whoa! Who is this guy with the tattoos, man?'."

But back to that New York hotel room. Nikki wasn't alone that night in being the subject of speculation from Dome. Tommy was having his own problems. His wife Heather was constantly calling him through the night, clearly hoping to catch him in some manner of illicit tryst. She must have thought she'd succeeded when on one occasion the unfortunate Julie, who just happened to be sitting by the phone, automatically picked it up.

Upon hearing a female voice on the end of her husband's phone Heather must have presumed the worst – or at least that's what Malcolm surmised from hearing Tommy's side of the subsequent, very loud, very animated conversation between husband and wife! It had a funny side, sure, but also suggested the marriage was far from the stable affair everybody had assumed. Whether Heather had good reason for this distrust, or whether it was paranoia based on Tommy's previous reputation, can only be speculated on. But this brief entrée into the world of Mötley Crüe circa '87 has subsequently convinced Dome that, with the benefit of hindsight, things were far from rosy back then – even if they were still great people to party with! Maybe even back then the band was beginning to fall apart at the seams.

58

Chapter Sixx - Girl Crazy

Nikki talks about the general chaos that reigned in the studio during the recording sessions for 'Girls, Girls, Girls'.

"We were such a mess, a complete disaster. Tom Werman probably saved that album. Songs like 'Dancing On Glass' and 'You're All I Need' were basically written in the studio, because we didn't have enough material. That was really sad, you know. One guy would be in Mexico getting his shit together while another guy was somewhere else getting wasted, and we just could never get all four together."

Still, like all good musicians promoting their new album, he tells *Kerrang!*'s Dante Bonutto at the time, "It's our best record ever. I'm like a proud papa. And what makes it so good is the fact that we're a seasoned rock'n'roll outfit now, a certified band... We've grown as a musical force, though I couldn't say that we've grown up!"

When 'Girls, Girls, Girls' is finally unveiled to the waiting public in May '87 it is warmly received. Malcolm Dome gives it a glowing review.

The album opens with the crushingly noisesome metal machinery of 'Wild Side', featuring one of the best riffs to flow from Mick Mars' streetwise arsenal. It's a sneering, violent gutter folk anthem boasting such telling couplets as: "*I carry my crucifix/Under my deathlist*". The title track follows, having a sleazy, easy heartbeat, yet also boasting a certain late '80s maturity.

"Every place has its own kind of women," Nikki explains in 1987. "Y'know, women can break up bands as well as split up best friends; the property that a chick has between her legs is really the most expensive there is... you can't live with 'em and you can't live without 'em." The song 'Girls, Girls, Girls' mirrors the above philosophy. It isn't just a paean to the glories of easy sex, but also has an underlying sense of impending menace. 'Dancing On Glass', meantime, draws heavily on Nikki's drug dependence:

"I've given up drugs now, and that's what the song's about," the bassist claims to Bonutto, convincing few that this was really the case. "I became a little too excessive in my habits and it started to hurt the music... Y'know people should really learn from the mistakes of others 'cos I've survived, but only just. I definitely could have been a casualty."

The song has a certain dark refrain, and is not so much a warning as to what might happen to you if you don't heed warnings about the demon of drugs, as virtually a plea from Nikki for help, understanding and support.

59

The simple line in the song that *"I've been thru' Hell/And I'm never goin' back"* wasn't so much a statement of intent as one born of fear. Sadly, few listened at the time with the right mental approach.

'Bad Boy Boogie' is a much more basic rock'n'roll entrapment, enlivened by some surprising rhythmic twists. But 'Nona' is a very personal, cathartic song from Sixx. Less than two minutes in length, it contains just one line, repeated over and over: *"Nona, I'm outta my head without you"*.

The 'Nona' is question is Nikki's grandmother. It was she who had brought him up and was arguably closer to him than anybody had been at the time. Her death in July 1986, it was claimed, had actually shaken Nikki out of his seemingly fatalistic fascination with heroin. Indeed, Sixx had been so strung out when she died that he couldn't even make it to the funeral. He was a pathetic figure.

"I was strung out bad for over a year," Nikki admitted late in '87. "I'd just bought a new house, and it turned into the Hollywood rock'n'roll headquarters... No-one can pull me out of anything once I start. I do what I want. I was probably trying to see how close to could get. Can I die... Heroin is the most dangerous drug. It's like heaven... and quitting hurts. Half the kids in LA are on junk. It's so fashionable, it scares the fuck out of me."
Considering that by the end of the year Nikki was to actually 'die' himself from shooting up, those words have the hollow ring of somebody who has convinced himself that he wanted to kick the habit, but was not yet strong enough to do so.

'Five Years Dead' again deals with the dangers of the rock'n'roll lifestyle, a preoccupation of Sixx's at the time it would seem. Nikki appears determined that others should realise what he'd been through, and is equally determined that the infamous PMRC (Parents Music Resource Center, run by one Tipper Gore, wife of future US Vice President Al Gore) should be aware of the manner in which he was tackling this thorny subject.

"I want some of those PMRC people to read the lyrics. (*'Five Years Dead'*) deals with the drinking, drugged, sex-crazed life of a rock'n'roll star who suddenly discovers what's happened to him."

Autobiographical to the max!

'All In The Name Of...' is a more typical Crüe youth anthem (*"For sex and sex I'd sell my soul"*), whilst 'Sumthin' For Nothin' again has a dark, debauched sense of its own freedom. Finally, as far as the Mötley originals go, there's 'You're All I Need'...

"It's about killing your girlfriend!" states Nikki. "I picked up the paper one day and I read about this guy who'd killed his girlfriend 'cos he couldn't stand to see her with another man. He'd have to kill her to make her his forever... If you love someone, hunt them down, and if they don't love you, kill them!"

This theme is explored subsequently by Guns N'Roses in the song 'I Used To Love Her, But I Had To Kill Her'. What this proved was that Mötley's perverse sense of humour was as intact as ever!

The album actually ends with a raucous, live rendering of 'Jailhouse Rock', recorded on the 'Theatre Of Pain' tour.

Overall, this is a magnificent affirmation of the Crüe. They take great strides both musically and lyrically, yet also retain their gross-out roots. And sonically, this was most confident offering yet from the band, producer Werman and engineer Baron stripping the sound down to the wire and then painstakingly rebuilding it into a colossus.

'Girls, Girls, Girls' is released at a time when metal is beginning seriously to dominate the US charts. Thanks to prolonged exposure on MTV, metal bands are now very much back in vogue. Big hair, leather and spandex is selling in droves. By the summer of '87, the top of the charts is simply riddled with top-notch hard rock. Whitesnake (revamped, and now effectively an American metal band) stands proudly at Number Two on the Billboard countdown with the seminal '1987' album (strange to think that the 'Snakes began their US sojourn that year in support of said album opening up for Mötley). Mötley themselves are entrenched at Number Three.

Just behind the Crüe stand management stablemates Bon Jovi and their landmark 'Slippery When Wet' offering, a record that was commercially to eclipse the Mötleys and reverse the two bands' relative standings with the McGhee organisation. Up until 'Slippery...', Mötley had been the kingpin. Now, the Jovis were to take over – and this was not going to amuse the Crüe. But more on that later.

Further down the charts lay up-and-coming LA heroes Poison, the first of a new generation to emerge from the sewers of the City Of Angels. Their second album, 'Open Up And Say... Ahh!' stands at Number Five, whilst hardy perennial Ozzy Osbourne rode hard at Number Six with his 'Tribute To Randy Rhoads' live effort. Everyone, it seems, wanted a piece of the metal action. With each passing week, new, exciting bands were emerging from every corner of the USA. Los Angeles was very much to the fore, thanks to Mötley more than anyone else. As their contemporaries such as Quiet Riot, Dokken and Ratt began to flounder and founder, the Crüe became stronger. They were truly the godfathers of the LA scene. (Oh, by the way, for the record, U2 topped the charts whilst all of this was going on).

It was indeed a wonderful time to be in the Crüe – or so it seemed. But there are one or two problems to surmount. For instance, the band hit trouble with the previously supportive MTV over the first three videos they shoot for songs from the album. The title cut, with its overt and explicit use of female flesh, is banned because of its sexist stance (strange that the likes of Madonna can comfortably get away with any form of libidinous behaviour in their videos, whilst rock bands such as Mötley Crüe run into a problems).

If this is not enough, 'Wild Side' creates a religious stir, because it's seen as lyrically raping the Lord's Prayer (presumably, objections were raised to the lines *"Thy kingdom come on the wild side/Our father who ain't in heaven/Be thy name on the wild side"*). Again, one must feel that if a 'serious' musician such as Bob Dylan had written something equally as 'blasphemous', then it would have been strenuously defended for being 'art'. However, Mötley Crüe are scuzzball rock'n'rollers who only incite rather than recite, and therefore can offer no social or religious comment beyond the superficially sensational. Fun, huh?
Finally, the storyline for 'You're All I Need' ensures that MTV treads very warily when it comes to airing that particular video. It's felt to be a little too perverse for the station's essentially young and impressionable audience. This situation, though, could only hit Mötley as a minor irritant compared to what's happening to them elsewhere.

Sadly they're forced to scrap much of their projected American tour because of Nikki's continuing health problems, brought on by his inability to live up to his previous public pronouncements and actually kick his drug habit. An official statement from the band's management blamed 'exhaustion' as the reason for the curtailment of touring commitments.

"Nobody believed that, did they?" Nikki says later, somewhat incredulous. "We never told anybody we were exhausted. We wanted to go *(to Europe for a tour)*, the management wouldn't let us. They go, 'If you guys go, we have to warn you that two members are not going to come back – you and Tommy are going to come home in a body bag!'."

Of course, all of this does have an amusing side. Mötley try to placate angry noises emanating from the UK about the cancellation of their tour by putting Mick on the phone to various journalists. They couldn't have made a worse choice. When asked to explain the reason behind Mötley's decision, Mick tells reporters that snow on the roof during the winter meant that venues couldn't take the weight of the extensive Crüe lighting rig hanging from the ceiling! Er, yes, well done Mick, thank you!

But what this situation underscores is just how serious things have become inside the Mötley enclave. Attempts to get Nikki to clean out in rehab after the 'Theatre Of Pain' tour had clearly failed. Now something drastic has to be done – and fast.

Chapter Seven
'All In The Name Of... Sixx?'

When 1988 began, nobody knew who the hell Matthew Trippe was – and nobody would have cared if he'd passed them on any street corner. Within a few weeks he had become inextricably linked with Mötley Crüe in general – and Nikki Sixx in particular.

Put simply, Matthew Trippe claimed that for a period of some two years he had been Nikki Sixx! In one of the most extraordinary stories of modern rock history, the strange case Matthew Trippe, Frank Ferrano and the character of Nikki Sixx unfolded like an oddball cousin of an Arthur Conan Doyle mystery before an increasingly incredulous public – not to mention a ravenous media. Basically, it was being maintained by Trippe that in mid-1983 Ferrano had been involved in a serious car crash and wasn't able to carry on with his career. In a desperate move to ensure that the momentum of the band wasn't impaired by this accident, it was alleged that Doc McGhee and Doug Thaler, the Mötley management team, decided to bring in a 'new' Nikki Sixx to replace the injured Ferrano, but this was to be done surreptitiously without the knowledge of anyone outside of the Mötley organisation.

They found one Matthew John Trippe, himself a bassist (having originally played guitar, before switching to the four strings) and someone with a striking physical resemblance to Ferrano. Trippe had by that point, he claims, already struck up a friendship with Mick Mars, whom he'd first met at The Troubadour Club earlier in 1983, soon after he'd arrived in Los Angeles from his home town of Erie, Pennsylvania. It was claimed by Trippe at the start of 1988 that he was brought into the band after being introduced to McGhee and Thaler by Mars and proving to their satisfaction that he was a competent musician.

Subsequently, Trippe (posing as Sixx) wrote the songs 'Danger' and 'Knock 'Em Dead Kid', credited under the name 'Nikki Sixx', for the album 'Shout At The Devil' and also performed live with the band on the corresponding tour. On August 28, 1984, Trippe was arrested in Erie on a charge of armed robbery.

This arrest dated back to an incident the previous April in Florida when Trippe had driven a friend, one John Spears, to a shop in order for the latter to purchase some beer. Whilst Trippe waited in the car, Spears held up the shopkeeper at knifepoint. Trippe, although he'd actually witnessed the incident, chose to ignore it and drove Spears away from the scene of the crime. It is then claimed that Trippe, following his arrest, returned to Florida, where he spent 39 days in jail, before Elektra apparently put up $50,000 in bail to spring him, so that he could continue to work on the 'Theatre Of Pain' album.

Trippe insisted that he then spent a month in the studio, from November 27, working on the 'Theatre...' sessions (he stated that he wrote 'City Boy Blues', 'Keep Your Eye On The Money' and 'Louder Than Hell') and that he subsequently appeared in the highly successful promotional video for 'Smokin' In The Boys' Room'.

Trippe was supposed to face trial in Florida on December 27 for his part in the aforementioned hold-up. Mick Mars drove him down there in his Ferrari, partly because the bassist had expressed an interest in buying that vehicle. But they never made it to Florida. Trippe decided to jump bail.

Four days later, the pair were actually caught for speeding by a local patrol car. Trippe, who was driving at the time, was fined $750. Apparently, the vehicle had been doing 189 mph in a zone with a speed limit of 45 mph – oops! But, fortunately for the bassist, the policemen who caught him for speeding didn't realise that he had jumped bail.

Matthew Trippe then decided to return home to Erie and hide out for a while at the house of a former professional associate. But on March 4, 1985, the police finally tracked him down. Because of the need for extradition proceedings to be processed between Pennsylvania and Florida, Trippe wasn't actually returned to the latter until June 28, when he was thrown back into jail until his trial. It was at this point, Trippe alleged, that McGhee and Thaler, increasingly nervous about their bassist's behaviour, chose to kick him into touch and contact Ferrano, now fully recovered, about rejoining the group. He accepted, went out on the 'Theatre Of Pain' tour – and they all lived happily ever after. Er, not exactly. According to the Trippe story, he was asked to carry on writing songs for the Crüe and all due royalties were to be placed in a trust fund for him until such time as he was released from jail.

Meantime, on August 13, 1985, Matthew Trippe finally came to trial on the armed robbery charge. On the advice of his lawyer, public defender David Mourik, he pleaded 'no contest' to the charge. He was subsequently returned to jail for a period of three months whilst various assessments were made before sentence could be passed. In November, Trippe was fined, received a six-month probation and was restricted for a period of two years to the Florida area (known as 'community control').

Trippe was moved to the drug rehabilitation centre known as The New Life Center for his two-year sentence. This place apparently looks to convert inmates into becoming Born Again Christians. They insist that persons in their charge must have their hair cut very short and can have no contact at all with the outside world.

However, Trippe by this time had developed a passionate fascination for Satanism. This had first reared its head on the 'Shout At The Devil' album, one that he had wanted to title 'Shout With The Devil'.

The title had been changed, claimed Trippe, because of management and record company fears that the original would create a backlash against the Crüe in conservative America.

Trippe was accepted into the Temple Of Set, an ancient Occult order, on Halloween 1985 – rather appropriate really. By November 1987, his community control sentence had run its due course and he was released – ready to cause huge problems for his alleged former colleagues.

It was at this juncture that he began to track down the royalties he claimed to be owed – only to find no trace. So his next step was to file a complaint citing 'civil theft' and 'other relief' against McGhee Enterprises Inc. and its principals Daniel 'Doc' McGhee and Douglas Thaler. In his deposition, Trippe alleged he had never received due royalties. He also wanted recognition for his part in the Mötley Crüe story.

Trippe insisted that he had written the aforementioned songs for 'Shout At The Devil' and 'Theatre Of Pain'. In addition, he maintained that the tracks 'Girls, Girls, Girls', 'All I Need', 'Dancing On Fire' (retitled 'Dancing On Glass') and 'Wild Side' from the 'Girls...' album were his copyright as well. This last batch, he said, were written whilst he was in jail.

Of course, neither McGhee nor Thaler took this suit particularly seriously, dismissing the claim out of hand and stating that Trippe was an impostor. But others were not so sure.

The story had originally been broken in the United States during January 1986 by *Runes*, the official magazine published by the Temple Of Set, although in their article they did make the mistake of writing that Trippe claimed to be the original Nikki Sixx. However, this whole story didn't get any wider media attention until two years later, when Trippe filed his lawsuit: presumably, until this happened anyone who did come across the story thought it to be the ramblings of a lunatic.

To back up his law suit, Trippe claimed that he had in his possession a piece of paper upon which he'd typed the first draft for the lyrics to a song called 'All I Need' (later he alleged this was retitled 'You're All I Need' for inclusion on the 'Girls...' album). It was suggested that chemical testing could prove they were written during the period 1984-5, at least two years before their appearance in public. Furthermore, *Kerrang!* ran a number of photos of Nikki Sixx during the so-called 'Ferrano periods' and the 'Trippe period', comparing the physical state of Nikki Sixx as it changed; they theorised as to whether it was possible to see any noticeable changes. No conclusion was reached.

The revelations were devastating. Although on the surface they were nothing more than the claims of a very odd individual, nonetheless the law suit was real enough. And there were those who began to wonder if this indeed could have some incredible basis in actuality.

Shortly after the suit was filed, *Kerrang!* managed to track down Trippe to put him on the spot, although just why the supposed Nikki Sixx granted an interview when the case was *sub judice*, and therefore no public comment could be passed on it by the parties involved, remains something of a mystery.

Trippe went into minute detail about how McGhee and Thaler, with the full knowledge and co-operation of Vince Neil, Tommy Lee and Mick Mars, constructed a new life for him as the replacement Nikki Sixx. How he had lived for a while at Tommy's apartment. How he had revamped the original songs for 'Shout At The Devil' ("When I heard those songs... I mean they really sucked. You should have heard 'Red Hot'. The vocals were right in the hole. And then I began to arrange breaks and timing and new words and clean them up. I would spice them up with Satanic references," he stated at one point to interviewer Ed Esposito).

But there are also distinct gaps and inconsistencies in his claims, which came through during the interview. For instance, at one point he says that he was sent out on a trip to promote the 'Shout At The Devil' album in America while, unbeknownst to him, Mötley were in Europe with Iron Maiden. Trippe alleges that Ferrano was brought back to play bass on this tour by McGhee, without his prior knowledge. Is it really likely that Mötley Crüe would be dumb enough to have Ferrano touring as Nikki Sixx at the same time as Trippe was playing the same role doing interviews with the media?!

Trippe goes on to state that he was in jail from August 28 until early September 1984, yet Nikki Sixx was seen out and about by a number of independent witnesses during this period! And surely, if Trippe had been fulfilling the role of Nikki Sixx then word about his original arrest would have got out to the media. There's no way that Nikki Sixx could have been jailed without somebody, somewhere in Florida getting to know about it.

During the course of his *Kerrang!* interview, Trippe dismisses 'Home Sweet Home' as a song he hated and had nothing to do with writing. So, why is Nikki Sixx credited with co-writing it? Surely the band weren't that anxious to fill their bassist's coffers, were they?

Furthermore, although Trippe claims to have first met Mick Mars just after the Us Festival in 1983, he believes that he wrote certain songs for the 'Shout...' album – which were actually aired at the festival!

The other incredible claim is that Trippe wrote 'Nona' – about Frank Ferrano's grandmother?! Is it likely? And if it was written by Trippe, who was the 'Nona' he referred to?

Finally, if this story were true, then it meant that a stand-in (Trippe) had successfully managed to fool Ferrano's closest family and friends. Or, that these people were privy to the whole conspiracy. Neither seems exactly convincing.

"I can honestly say that I was never approached to become part of any conspiracy concerning Nikki," stated an adamant Robbin Crosby when confronted at the time on this thorny subject. "That means if this is true, then I saw two different Nikkis over a period of a couple of years and never noticed. I admit that I was fucked-up for some of the time, but I think I would still have noticed something like that."

No argument there!

There was, though, a certain degree of limited validity to Trippe's tale, at least insofar as Nikki was involved in a car crash during June 1983. But that fact was never hidden by the Mötley camp anyway, and was a matter of public knowledge.

Doug Thaler, obviously seething about this whole situation and the way the media had seemingly given credence to Trippe's claim, had this to say when contacted by *Kerrang!* shortly after the story first broke:

"I don't know if it was Trippe who initiated this bullshit in publications in England, which has also spread throughout Europe, but it's bloody annoying. I would be happy to set you straight, except for one thing – this clown Trippe's suing us! Let them come to court and then the truth will come out"

Nikki Sixx himself (well, the Frank Ferrano model) commented as follows: "We got this deposition – this fat kid in sunglasses. I guess you can say you're anybody. I've had fans come to my house and go, 'Nikki, is this true?'. No, it's absolutely not true. It's creepy, though. It's like when John Lennon died and you got all those fucking weirdos.

"I'm not paranoid or anything, but now I not only live in a gated community, I have gates around my house and a massive alarm system, and I have loaded machine guns. It may sound like full paranoia, but that Matthew Trippe guy bummed my life out... The thing is, how do I know that he's not out to get me? It could very well happen. The guy even copied my tattoos, which is really bizarre.

"You know why it got to me? Because somebody brought it to my attention about a year ago. They said, 'Nikki, do you realise that the guy who killed John Lennon thought he was John Lennon?', and I said, 'What are you trying to tell me?'. Their answer was, 'Watch your ass'... He *(Trippe)* is on acid. You know, the guy's been in mental institutions."

75

76

Eventually, after numerous postponements and even a false report in November 1989 that the case had been thrown out, Trippe finally dropped his law suit on December 10 1993, and has disappeared back to the anonymity whence he came. Not, however, without leaving a certain amount of mental scar tissue on Nikki. Maybe, Trippe did believe in his own story. Perhaps he was trying to get cheap publicity for his own band, Sixx Pack (who actually fired him anyway). Whatever, he created enough waves in the Mötley camp for the name to remain a source of horror even to this day.

But, strangely enough, those very publications in the UK that first brought this whole matter to the fore failed to report when Trippe lost his case. Interesting. It isn't only Nikki who's at the centre of litigation in 1988. Doc McGhee is arrested in January on a charge of helping to smuggle 40,000lbs of marijuana into North Carolina from Columbia. It's a charge dating back to 1982, prior to Mötley signing their deal with McGhee Enterprises.

When the case finally comes to court, McGhee pleads guilty. But to everyone's surprise, for the second time in a matter of three years, someone connected with the Mötley Crüe camp is let off quite lightly on a serious charge.

In 1985, it had been Vince Neil who was the centre of adverse attention, now it was McGhee. He receives a five year suspended prison sentence, is fined a derisory $15,000 and is also ordered to set up an anti-drugs foundation. This foundation eventually takes on the name of 'Make A Difference' and will raise money in 1989 through two high profile concerts in Moscow and the compilation album 'Stairway To Heaven/Highway To Hell'. Many were angry that McGhee's money and position had allowed him effectively to escape a long prison term. But, it was obviously felt that he was best able to serve out his sentence by helping the community at large to fight the prevalent drug problem.

The 'Make A Difference' shows in Moscow will actually signal the end of the relationship between Mötley and McGhee. But that's in the future. In the meantime, there's some good news for the band in 1988 amidst all this controversy and heartache. Vince Neil marries his girlfriend Sharise in April (his second marriage). They met when she was working as a mud wrestler at the Tropicana Club in Los Angeles. Mind you, she herself would become the cause of headlines in 1989 – and not exactly for the right reasons either!

Chapter Eight
Give Peace A Chance

1989. Mötley Crüe are straight. Drink-free, drug-free straight. Indeed, Tommy Lee is taking this straight business so much to heart that he's spotted at a Barry Manilow concert in May! (Remember, he met Heather Locklear at an REO Speedwagon concert, so who knows who he hoped to find at this one...)

They say the groupies in LA don't hang out at the Rainbow or the Cat House any more; they're all down at Alcoholics Anonymous and Narc Anon meetings, because that's where you go these days if you want to run into a rock star. Everyone's straightening up, all the rock bands. The heavier they were, the straighter they're getting. Strange days...

Nikki: "I do feel it is a bit of a bandwagon, to be honest with you. But I didn't get sober so I could join another fucking bandwagon. I did it because I was waking up every day and shooting smack into my arm and drinking whisky just so I could get through the day.

"I don't like the preaching aspect of the AA or NA or CA (cocaine abuse) programme. I don't really go to meetings because I'm a very private person and I don't like people to talk to me in general. And I resent people going, 'Hey Nikki, how you doing, buddy?'. Who the fuck are you to call me 'buddy', just because you've got a drug problem and I've got a drug problem and you're at a meeting? I think a lot of bands go there just to to meet other bands.
"It's a bit fucked-up of me, but I don't really care. I suppose if someone's there trying to get sober I should be supportive, but I'm not really, because I don't trust anybody. I'm like the asshole of AA!"

Nikki cleaned up – Mötley cleaned up – for one reason and one reason only. Music. Caught up in the excessive rock musician lifestyle, they've started to let the actual rock music bit fall by the wayside.

Nikki: "I'm a musician first and foremost. I'm an entertainer second. I used to think I was an entertainer first and a musician second, but the music is so important to me. I don't want to be thought of as a Kiss, with no validity after how many years – 15 years? – to get there. We're coming up to our ninth year together. I expect respect. And the only way I can demand it is by respecting myself and my own music.

"So I've had to change a few things. And one of the things I've had to change was the fact that every morning I'd wake up and have to cook up a spoon of smack and a spoon of coke just to get me to the bathroom so I could throw up for my morning puke. That isn't how I thought I was going to take my music seriously.

"I had no intention of giving up, just so I could become another rock'n'roll tragedy, like a Sid Vicious meets Jim Morrison in *Rebel Without A Cause*. Fuck man, I haven't even hit my prime yet musically. So I said, I've got to get my shit together – even if it's only temporarily; I can't say how long I can do this – and make the best, most kick-ass music ever. That's what I'm on this planet to do."

So it's a straight Crüe that flies out to the Soviet Union to appear at the Moscow Music Peace Festival in August, the concert that started life in an American courtroom where manager Doc McGhee was sentenced, in bizarre American courtroom fashion, to organising a major fund and awareness-raising event for the Make A Difference Foundation, specifically set up to deal with alcohol and substance abuse.

The line-up for the two identical shows is Mötley, Skid Row, Cinderella, Ozzy Osbourne, Scorpions and Bon Jovi, plus dodgy Russian rock bands Nuance, Brigada S and Gorky Park. They've chartered a jet – dubbed in best Woodstockian fashion 'The Magic Bus' – which will take off from New York, destination Moscow, with a planeload of rock'n'rollers, stopping on the way in London and Germany to pick up the rest of the performers.

A slight hitch. Someone phones the authorities in New York and says he's planted a bomb on the plane. Everyone and everything has to come off while the sniffer dogs go to work. The dogs probably had a serious hangover the next morning...

So join us 30,000 feet above solid ground where there's a party going on! Jon Bon Jovi, Richie Sambora, Tom Keifer of Cinderella, Ozzy Osbourne's Zakk Wylde, have all got their guitars out and are jamming in the back row on old Stones and Eagles songs. Stowaway Jason Bonham (son of the late Led Zeppelin drummer) is accompanying them on the table top. In the front row the musicians are taking bets on exactly how much of the ozone layer the MTV VJ singlehandedly destroyed with the amount of hairspray he had on his head. And, passing the length of the aeroplane and back, various bags and bottles. Sebastian Bach waggishly renames the event the Make A Different Drink Foundation!

"I was drunk the whole time," Sebastian tells Sylvie backstage in Moscow. "Everybody was. Except Mötley Crüe."

And there was plenty to drive the band to drink. For a start, the Crüe's crew still aren't given their visas until the day before the show; they miss their plane to Moscow and, when they do get here, are almost refused entry to the country. Not to mention the fact that Moscow itself would make an alcoholic of the Archbishop of Canterbury. It's certainly had that effect on the Russians.

Russia. You know the preconceptions: cockroach-ridden stalags, grey wretched people, men in trenchcoats mumbling into their sleeves, soldiers everywhere, no food except variations on Spam, no anything unless you bribe with American dollars and packets of cigarettes (Marlboro preferred) – well, that was just the hotel... The Hotel Ukraine, Moscow's top flop-house – commissioned by the late dictator Stalin and apparently still run by his close personal friends – is home from home for the week for Bon Jovi, Ozzy, Scorpions, Skid Row, Cinderella and the Crüe. Sensibly, the Western bands bring over their own caterer and 75 tons of food, from teabags to tacos, in a smart Spam-avoidance plot. Even the Hard Rock Café fly in and set up an open-air burger bar in Moscow's Gorky Park.

The walk through the park to Lenin Stadium, where the festival takes place, is a very strange one. No people, no bottles, not so much as a scrap of paper – very un-festivalish – just lots of trees with hidden speakers playing chirpy cartoon music. Just past the huge statue of Lenin is the stadium they built to hold the 1980 Olympic Games. Ten years old, its general state of dilapidation makes it look far older. Crumbling steps, medieval toilets.

The only immaculate part is the pitch, where the festival crowd will stand. It's covered with tarpaulins and astroturf. It's also covered with soldiers.

For a 'peace' festival, there are a hell of a lot of guys in uniform packing guns. A 300-man unit of Gorbachev's finest in sweatpants and T-shirts making a wall around the stage, holding hands so that not so much as a breath could pass through. Then, in front of them, two rows of blue uniformed militia with cotton wool in their ears. Down the middle, separating the stadium into two parts like the bone in a T-bone steak, a line of benches with green-uniformed army men sitting close together, facing alternate directions. And in the first and second rows of the seated section, all the way around the stadium, two rows of militia. Oh yes, and cops at every exit. When Ozzy asked for some water – you know how he likes to chuck the stuff around – evidently the Russians thought he was unhappy with the low level of security and gave him a high-powered riot-situation firehose!

With the eyes of the world upon them – a number of international TV crews have their cameras focused on the proceedings – the Soviet authorities aren't taking any chances. They even seed the clouds the day before the show to make sure there's no rain to mar the event.

The stadium is nowhere near filled to its maximum 100,000 capacity. Not for lack of interest. A smaller audience is more manageable. A specially-selected audience is even more manageable. On the first day, the crowd looks more like people with friends in high places than vodka-swilling, black-market-jeans-wearing rock fans.

At 1.15 on a sunny afternoon they light the Olympic torch, for the first time since 1980, and Skid Row hit the stage. And what a stage they hit! Two hundred and eighty six feet wide, 120 feet deep. There are 2000 lights and 200 speaker cabinets, with a diamond video screen showing close-ups on one side. Sebastian Bach naturally proceeds to inspect the entire area as fast as possible, camera crews in hot pursuit.

"The whole point of this show today," he yells, "is to have East meet West and kick some ass!"

The Skids get a 35-minute set. From Cinderella on it's 55 minutes each. But first there are three Russian bands. Nuance, Russia's third most popular act, look and sound like ageing LA session men. Brigada S go in for big Germanic '70s art school posturing. Gorky Park, with their see-through pants and long red coats, are the first Russian longhairs and play Western metal mixed with Russian folk.

Cinderella play an excellent set – backstage after the show, several bands vote them best band of the day.

And then, the Crüe. Their first ever straight show. The first time, as Nikki confesses backstage to Sylvie, that the band had ever set foot onstage drink and drug-free. They're all nervous, he says. They needn't have been. They're in excellent form. Even the subdued first-day crowd likes them, and 'Shout At The Devil' manages to drown out the racket of the Aeroflot helicopter hovering overhead.

Vince is in great voice since giving up the bottle – in good physical form, too, from the way he clambers up to the top of the video screen in 'Looks That Kill' and tries to get the crowd to sing along. The Russians aren't too big on joining in, especially when asked to yell 'Fuck yeah!'. Then the backing girls Nasty Habits come out, squeezed into sexy tight leather – the po-faced soldiers start to twitch – and help out on 'Smokin' In The Boys' Room', 'Girls, Girls, Girls' and 'Jailhouse Rock'. Vince asks the audience if they've heard of Elvis Presley. They don't answer. At the end of the set, Nikki pulls Tommy's drum kit down on top of him, and smashes his bass into smithereens, throwing the bits to the crowd. The next day outside the show, fragments of guitar are changing hands on the blackmarket at some serious prices.

84

So, an excellent and successful set from Mötley. But Ozzy's really the man the crowd have been waiting for – among the banners and flags, one Russian, several American and a Kiss Army flag of all things, are several bearing his name. They've been chanting his name since the beginning of the show, and noticeably liven up when he comes on. Second in the Russian popularity stakes are the Scorpions, since they've played Russia before, and since – ever the professionals – they've learned some Russian words and a Russian folk song which the crowd loves them for. They have the one magic moment of the first day's show: as the introduction to 'Still Loving You' rings out, a sudden gust of wind sucks the Olympic torch high into the night sky, girls sit on their boyfriends' shoulders, matches are lit around the stadium, and even some of the army take off their caps and wave them along in time to the music.

Bon Jovi arrive in style – Jon dressed in a Red Army cap and coat and marching right up the middle of the crowd, then leaping onto the stage. Laser beams cut the night. A flashbin explodes. The band are on brilliant form. So brilliant that someone even tosses a toilet roll onstage. A true accolade. Toilet rolls are so scarce in Moscow you could probably swap one on the black market for a car. And so day two dawns. Mick Mars is sitting at a table in the catering hall nursing what looks suspiciously like a beer, a black look on his face. The Peace Festival atmosphere is starting to turn noticeably bellicose.

Bon Jovi and the Crüe are about to declare war. Ozzy is ready to walk out. The Ozzy situation started before he'd even landed on Russian soil – his wife and manager Sharon Osbourne pulled the plug when TV ads for the event in the States featured all of Doc McGhee's bands but barely mentioned Ozzy. She's persuaded to reconsider.

And then, in Moscow, the show's running order is changed behind Ozzy's back, putting him onstage before Mötley Crüe – a pretty crazy situation considering his obviously superior status with the Russians. Ozzy and Sharon decide to split.

As the couple are packing to fly home the night before the show, a visit from Doc McGhee at three in the morning, promising a return to the original bill, manages to save the day.

Except that no-one has dared to tell the Crüe.

When they finally find out, on the morning of the show, they refuse to swap positions. So Ozzy and Sharon pack up and go. As they're leaving, they literally bump into Jon Bon Jovi in the corridor. He offers Ozzy Bon Jovi's slot on the bill, as headliner.

87

"This show," Jon tells Sylvie, "was supposed to be all for one and one for all, but it turned into an ego thing. Ozzy wouldn't go on before Mötley and Mötley wanted to go on after Ozzy and Ozzy threatened to walk, and we had agreed to close the show. The second night I said, look man, I'll be happy to trade with Ozzy and go on fourth from the top, no problem. To be honest with you, the Scorpions kicked our ass the night before anyway..."

Oh yes, the night before. Another problem. Bon Jovi used pyro. They were at the top of the bill using pyro. Mötley were fourth on the bill and they weren't allowed to use pyro. Their manager wasn't standing up for them in the battle of the bands. Doc McGhee was plainly favouring his new stars, Bon Jovi, over his old band Mötley Crüe. A heated discussion ensues. Tommy Lee's fist finds itself in the general area of Doc McGhee's face.

Jon Bon Jovi: "What happened was that when I walked down that centre aisle in a Russian soldier's suit, they thought that it was a set-up. And then somebody somehow knocked over one piece of pyro – truly in my heart of hearts it was an accident – it just happened to go off, and as this thing happened we opened our show. And I knew what we were going to do that second night. Apparently Mötley got really mad and Tommy punched Doc McGhee. I've never spoken to him about the incident, but that's the truth. I just had to think of some way not to get blown off by the Scorpions two nights in a row – and we didn't the second night!"

The second show, despite the backstage battles, is infinitely better than the first one. Same sets, same songs, but somehow it's more real. The audience look like real fans, the weather's more real too – a downpour. The crowd pull up the astroturf and hold it over their heads. The militia get bored standing there in the rain and smash a couple of heads with truncheons.

And the bands go on in exactly the same order as they did yesterday, Bon Jovi headlining. And at the end, various musicians appear for the jam session: 'Hound Dog', 'Long Tall Sally', 'Back In The USSR' and Zeppelin's 'Rock'N'Roll' – Jason Bonham playing drums alongside Randy Castillo of Ozzy's band. Doc McGhee and co-organiser Stas Namin (head of the Moscow Peace Committee) come up too and everyone join hands singing 'Give Peace A Chance', tossing flowers into the crowd as fireworks explode into the Moscow sky. Everyone except Ozzy – no-one knows where he is – and Jon Bon Jovi, who's gone off to take a pee.

By the end of the 'peace' festival, the band have split for ever with McGhee. They're now managed by his former partner, Doug Thaler.
Still, backstage, everyone is talking about how amazing the new substance-free Crüe is. Several rock'n'rollers, Sebastian Bach of course chief among them, have been doing their damnedest to tempt the Mötleys off the wagon and see if the talk of clean-up is all hype. They don't succeed. Not even Sebastian.

"You might think, 'Oh Sebastian's on the road with fucking Mötley, he's giving them drugs and drinking with them and all this shit'. I tried! They just have no desire.

"I partied with them before they went straight, and when they said they would die that's no shit. Did you ever party with Mötley back then? Then you know those motherfuckers ain't poser partiers. They don't say 'I'm a bad boy rock'n'roller. I have a sip of beer once a week'. Those fucking guys did rails this big every fucking day, spelled their names out in it – heroin, crack, all that shit – and that was a part of their lives. They're very strong. They drink a lot of non-alcoholic beer though. Like all day, that's all they drink."

Fred Coury of Cinderella concurs:
"Mötley won't do anything at all now. The Mötleys used to be nuts and they cleaned it up, and when you hear their new record you'll be blown way. It's their best album by far – not just a little bit better, it's a mind-blower! Which just goes to prove that when you've got a straight head you can think so much better."

They've been recording their first drug-free album in Little Mountain Studio in Vancouver with new producer Bob Rock. Its title: 'Dr. Feelgood'.

Nikki: "We moved into these one bedroom apartments up there. It rained every day, drove me crazy. I can't handle the rain all the time; that's why I left Seattle. Aerosmith was in one studio while we were in the other, and Gorky Park was in one and another time The Cult was in. Everybody came and went while we were there. God, man, six months in the studio. Our first album took seven days! It took us a year to write it."

It wasn't being straight that took them so long – when Ozzy Osbourne cleaned up he said the hardest thing was trying to come up with new songs without alcoholic inspiration – at least according to Nikki, so much as deciding what direction to take the huge amount and variety of material that was surfacing. A lot of what he used to call "spontaneity" – like the 'Girls, Girls, Girls' album, which took him all of three weeks to write, "five minutes each song, no thought put into them at all" – was in fact an excuse for being so wasted that he couldn't get out of his house and down to rehearsals.

"What we did this time is we took a really really open mind and decided to record anything that came to mind. It was really cool. We recorded a rap song – that was the most bizarre song called 'Monstrous', which I really liked. It was like LL Cool J or – I hate to say it – like the Beastie Boys."

There was talk at one point of it turning up on the soundtrack to *Ghostbusters 2*. "And this song is only about a minute and a half long and it goes directly into this other song called 'Say Yeah', which might have been about ten minutes long with this bizarre Pink Floyd/'Whole Lotta Love' space stuff going on in the middle – completely experimental stuff. Me and Tommy stayed up for two days in the studio doing backwards tape and all kinds of effects we could think of, harmonised guitars going backwards.

"It never ended up on the album. It was just the fact that we were trying anything and everything. We recorded 20 or more songs. And that's why the album took so long to do.

"I actually spent a month writing the lyrics this time. I'm not sure if it makes it better or worse, because I've changed them like a hundred times. They'd go, 'We're going to sing 'Dr. Feelgood' today', and I'd go, 'I'll be right back!'. And I'd go back to the hotel and zzzzzp! I'd change them, 'Yeah, okay, these will work'. I just wanted to get more into a Phil Lynott or an Ian Hunter style of writing, really colourful stories.

"There's this song I'm very happy with lyrically *(the title track)* which is about this kid named Jimmy who's a hoodlum, and as the song progresses he becomes the King of the Streets. And he goes from the barrio up to Shangri La, living in this Mediterranean mansion. And he has the girls and the limos and the machine guns and the piles of cocaine, and in the end he gets blown away. And then he used to be the one they called Dr. Feelgood. That's like a real great story and the video follows along that line. We figured we were going to get the video banned, since our last three videos have been banned!"

They've changed producer, from Tom Werman to Bob Rock. "He's perfect," says Nikki. "He's like 35, in our mental space, he grew up with Zeppelin and Humble Pie and the Faces. He had a band called the Payolas – he's a good musician, versatile, plays all the different instruments. He opened up our minds a lot." (In fact Rock plays bass on the track 'Time For Change' while Nikki plays keyboards.)

Robin Zander and Rick Nielsen of Cheap Trick guest on 'She Goes Down'. Steven Tyler of Aerosmith, Jack Blades of Damn Yankees, Bob Rock and Bryan Adams sing back-up vocals on 'Sticky Sweet'. Skid Row join in the general background noise on 'Time For A Change'. The album, simply, rocks. Released in September it goes Top Five in Britain. Better yet, in the US it's their first album to make it to Number One.

'Dr. Feelgood' marks another major step in the development of Mötley Crüe. Sonically, it is a departure from anything they've previously undertaken, having a slightly harsher edge. And the songs are arguably more developed and intricate. Certainly, working with Bob Rock seems to have matured the band considerably. Perhaps being free of Tom Werman plays its part.

Whatever, the album curiously isn't as immediate as what has gone before. It takes several plays actually to get into the songs – but it all proves worthwhile in the long run. The songs are well constructed and, although they offer nothing dramatically new, nonetheless they spectacularly showcase a band in complete control of themselves and their studio environment.

The likes of the title track and 'Slice Of Your Pie' provide for a mid-tempo pace, with the rhythmic succulence of the foursome well to the fore. 'Kickstart My Heart' and 'Rattlesnake Shake' each in their own way up the velocity, whilst 'Same Ol' Situation (S.O.S.)' and 'She Goes Down' keep up a partying atmosphere, thereby proving that the Mötleys certainly haven't sacrificed any of their bonhomie in the search for credibility.

Of course, there is a ballad present. However, 'Without You' isn't a syrupy embarrassment, as is the case with so many bands who just record ballads because they know they're easy to chart, and consequently help to sell the album.

The overall feel of this 11 song extravaganza is of a band striding purposefully out of the '80s and towards a new decade offering fresh challenges. 'Dr. Feelgood' also seems like an album that is closing one era, whilst beckoning the listener through to a new, equally exciting and unpredictable one. Musically, just where would Mötley take their fans in the coming years?

In September, the same month that 'Dr. Feelgood' is released, Mötley have been invited to present the prize in the heavy metal category at the annual MTV Awards.

Which is where Vince Neil punches out Guns N'Roses guitarist Izzy Stradlin. The second Crüe fisticuffs display in less than two months happens in a corridor backstage. Guns are there to play a number. Izzy, allegedly, was getting too friendly with Vince's wife Sharise, or maybe Sharise was getting too friendly with him, depends who's telling the story. As the Guns come offstage, Vince jumps on the guitarist.

The incident starts a long-running feud between the two bands. Guns vocalist Axl, especially, never misses an opportunity to say the Crüe are crap. At one point he starts wearing a T-shirt reading 'Mötley' with a red line through it. But there's work to be done. The Crüe are getting ready for the 'Dr. Feelgood' world tour. They warm-up with a secret show at the tiny Whisky club under their by now well-known pseudonym, The Fourskins.

December finds them playing a sell-out show at the huge Meadowlands Arena in New Jersey. Their first single (the title track) is in the American Top Ten, their album is at the top and well on its way to going quadruple platinum. And another album featuring the Crüe comes out.

93

'Stairway To Heaven/Highway To Hell' – the final effort of Doc McGhee's
Make A Difference Foundation to raise funds and awareness about drink and
drugs – features all of the bands on the Moscow bill covering a track by a band
who've had a member die of substance abuse. Bon Jovi play Thin Lizzy's 'The
Boys Are Back In Town', The Scorpions do The Who's 'Can't Explain', Ozzy
Osbourne tackles Jimi Hendrix's 'Purple Haze' and Mötley Crüe cover (the late
Deep Purple and James Gang guitarist) Tommy Bolin's 'Teaser'.

Nikki: "'Teaser'... anything Bolin put his fingerprints on is amazing. When he
died it was one of the saddest moments in history. He never really got to do
what he was supposed to do."

And the Moscow festival cast – which also includes Cinderella, Skid Row,
Gorky Park and Jason Bonham – get together to sing the songs featured in the
festival's encore: 'Hound Dog', 'Whole Lotta Shakin' Going On' and
'Rock'N'Roll'. A lasting testament to a year of peace...

Chapter Nine
Happiness Is A Warm Gun

After the shock waves which have been spreading through the Mötley camp over the previous few years, the band could certainly have done with the comparative calm that is to settle over their activities during the first year of the new decade.

There is to be no new product from them, as they're busy working on a special compilation album that is to see the light of day the following year, released to coincide with celebrations of the foursome's tenth year together.

With a Number One album in America at last under their collective belts in 'Dr. Feelgood' ("It was a great feeling... orgasmic," Nikki tells *Kerrang!* shortly after the album reached the top of the charts), the various members could afford to take a breather after the huge accompanying tour and begin to contemplate future solo projects.

Nikki talks openly – albeit not for the first time – about publishing a book of his poetry (tentatively titled *The Education Of Rebellion*, this tome has still to see the light of day as you read this. Yet it has been a passion of Nikki's for some while and something he has continually mentioned during interviews over a period of some years). He also suggests that Mick wanted to perform jazz fusion music in the vein of the great Jeff Beck! Here's what he tells *Kerrang!* about that poetry book and also Mick's project early in 1990:

"Maybe the one thing we can't do in Mötley Crüe is go so far into an extreme like doing jazz or a whole fusion thing. I know Mick would like to get into some instrumental stuff and some fusion stuff *à la* Jeff Beck, so he might go out and do a solo album. I'd love to see him do it.

"*(When I write lyrics)* they have to be formed to the music and to the band, whereas image-wise without those constraints I'd be a lot darker and lot more devious in my writing... By doing my book I won't have to do anything even a little to the left or right of what I want to do exactly... This book is something I've always wanted to do."

Even back in early 1990, Mötley have already decided that no new studio album would emerge from the mother ship until 1993, thereby allowing the four Mötleys to explore other areas of creative activity.

Vince is follow up his cameo role in the comedy *Police Academy VI* the previous year with a small part in *The Adventures Of Ford Fairlane*, a vehicle designed around the hard-hitting comedic talents of arguably the hottest and most controversial comedian in America at this time, Andrew Dice Clay. Vince is cast as a rock'n'roll singer who dies onstage. Hmmm.

Mötley also take time out to record a new song for the soundtrack of this movie – a little something titled 'Rock'N'Roll Junkie'. This is also to appear on the forthcoming compilation album.

Meanwhile, outside of the band both Nikki and Mick are invited to guest on the new Alice Cooper album 'Hey, Stoopid!', along with a plethora of other star names. It's almost an affirmation of their acceptance at the very highest level of rock music – no longer could they just be dismissed as... well, rock'n'roll junkies. Alice has been at the pinnacle of his profession for some 15 years. Now here he is acknowledging the next generation of major players.

In addition, the ubiquitous Tommy takes time out to guest on two projects. First he is asked by top bassist Stu Hamm to get behind the kit for one track on his third solo album; Hamm had made his name as the four-stringer in Joe Satriani's band. Then, as if this wasn't enough to raise eyebrows towards the ceiling, Lee turns up on an album from soft-rocker Richard Marx.

Tommy: "He wanted a really heavy drummer, right. Then I heard who he was working with. Steve Lukather. He's a fucking unbelievable fucking guitarist. He plays nothing like he does when he's with his band *(Toto)*. A really heavy, radical guitar player."

All of these records are to see the light of day during 1991 and will be looked at in slightly greater detail when we come to that particular year. But, given the comparatively light workload taken on by the band, various thoughts turn towards women – specifically to marriage. This is the year when Mick marries Mötley backing singer Emi Canyn (his second marriage). Emi is one of the Nasty Habits, the female backing duo first introduced to the world on the 'Girls...' tour (the other member of this elite is Donna McDaniel). In addition, Nikki is finally led down the aisle by Brandi Brandt, whom he's been dating virtually since the break-up of his relationship with Vanity.

Nikki gets married during May and is to become a father on January 25, 1991, when his son Gunnar is born. How times change. All four Mötleys are now married, if not exactly settled into the slipper 'n' pipe routine. But this domestic bliss is not to last for very long, though that's another story further along this particular happy trail.

Nikki also speaks to *Kerrang!*, at length at this time, about his supposed interest in the Occult, often rumoured yet never fully broached before. He admits:

"There was a short time when me and Lita *(Ford)* were living together *(the early '80s)* and the band had just done 'Too Fast For Love' and were gearing up for

97

'Shout At The Devil' and I got interested in black magic and voodoo. "We were interested – but we weren't into it... We were kids, we were high and curious... I get interested in everything from people's habits to computers to cars to guns – and black magic was one of those things. It was dark, it was taboo – then it was boring. Maybe I didn't search deep enough, and maybe that's a good thing."

During this period as well, both Nikki and Tommy have discovered a mutual fascination with guns – in particular machine guns. Whilst making the 'Dr. Feelgood' album the pair would, says Nikki, "Go out into the desert and just fire the machine guns. That made us feel sooo good, y'know. It's another form of getting high without using drugs.

"I got into guns at this stage for the sheer and utter power... I was into the loudest gun that shot the loudest bullets. I've got an arsenal of weapons at home... If war ever breaks out in southern California then I'm prepared." Tommy concurs. "Drinking and drugs is such a shallow thing in our life compared with what there is to do out there! I can walk into this room in my home – I live out in the country – open my safe, grab a fucking couple of machine guns, and just annihilate shit that I've got set up on a target outside. Or I can come back inside and fuck my wife until I fall over, or ride one of my bikes. When you're all hungover and fucked-up, you don't want to do any of that shit."

Inevitably, controversy is never far away from tapping them on the shoulder or spitting right in their eye. Come on, this is Mötley Crüe; what do you expect? The feud with Guns N'Roses seems to be escalating almost weekly into a full-scale nuclear holocaust with accusations and counter-accusations, threats and counter-threats. Axl Rose tells Mick Wall of *Kerrang!*:

"Izzy never touched that chick *(Vince's wife)*. If anybody tried to hit on anything, it was her trying to hit on Izzy when Vince wasn't around... The whole story is that Vince took a pot-shot at Izzy when he was walkin' offstage at the MTV Awards... because Vince's wife has got a bug up her ass about Izzy."

When Axl challenges Vince Neil with the statement that, "Vince, whichever way you want it, man: guns, knives or fists. I don't care, whatever you want to do... I wanna see that plastic face of his caved in", Nikki hits back by maintaining: "Izzy fucked with Vince's wife, so Vince punched him out. And if Axl doesn't shut up, he's going to start something, too."

Vince also has a verbal lash at the Guns N'Roses singer:

"I only speak out against people who fuck me over, whereas someone like Axl gets on the soapbox about everything and everybody in the world.
When I punched Izzy, Axl made a whole bunch of lies about it and made a big

deal out of the whole story... Funny thing was, you never heard from Izzy... because he knew exactly what happened. Now Axl has said a bunch of stuff about Nikki. It's a shame, Axl used to be a nice guy."

Before this story is to run its course, Vince is to go on MTV and challenge Axl to a fight (this, to the best of the authors' knowledge, has yet to take place. Maybe they should get Don King involved?). And Axl was to create a huge fuss in London at a Guns N'Roses post-Wembley Stadium gig party in 1991, which both authors attended, when someone inadvertently put on a Mötley Crüe album. The singer demanded that the record was removed – instantly. Or heads would roll.

If the GN'R situation showed little sign of dying down, then the tension between Mötley and former management stablemates Bon Jovi is equally as great.

Tommy elects to tell the world what he thinks of Bon Jovi in general – and Jon Bon in particular – towards the middle of 1990, nearly a full year after the infamous Moscow Music Peace Festival.

"I remember when Jon Bon Jovi was nothing, nobody knew who the fuck the kid was. He was begging Doc McGhee, 'Please, please let me hang out with the Crüe! Let me spend just a couple of days on the bus. I want to see what a real tour is like'. So, Johnny comes out with us, we showed him the ropes of the road. We put him on our bus, get him fucked-up by this bunch of girls, get him drunk... show him what the arenas are like. He was just like, 'Wow, this is great'.

"Then the fucking guy has some success and all of a sudden he won't talk to us. All of a sudden we're dickheads. Well, fuck that guy, man! We showed him what rock'n'roll is all about!"

The Crüe certainly know how to pick their enemies. No shrinking violets for them. They may have now cleaned out their bodies, trading Evian water for Jack Daniel's, but there was no mistaking the fact that the fire and passion still burns deep within them.

Talking of passions, Vince takes advantage of this lull in Crüe commitments to indulge a burgeoning pastime: motor racing. While he may never have been able to challenge Nigel Mansell on the circuit, nonetheless Neil throws himself into this comparatively new hobby (his interest dates back to the mid-'80s) with considerable gusto, taking part not only in celebrity races, but also in more serious competition whenever he can.

At the time, it all seems like harmless fun. However, within a couple of years this is to prove a major bone of contention between the singer and the rest of the band, indirectly playing its part in their eventual split.

99

Chapter Ten – Decadence Within

appy anniversary! This year Mötley Crüe celebrate their tenth anniversary – and who would have thought all those years ago that such an event would occur?! Near death experiences, doppelgangers, overdoses – the band have survived all of this and more during their turbulent time together.

Of course, these days every band – major or otherwise – tends to mark such occasions with a significant resurrection of their back-catalogue. For some it comes in the form of a boxed set, featuring not only alternative takes of classic material, but also songs consigned years previously to the cutting room floor – and usually with good reason. But Mötley content themselves with 'Decade Of Decadence'.

The idea behind 'Decade Of Decadence' is to draw together a coherent compilation of tracks covering the Mötleys' entire career to date, as well as to add in certain bonuses, which means comparative rarities and even new recordings.

But all of this, while still ongoing, won't be surfacing until October. Before that time, much would occur to the band.

Early in the year, Stu Hamm issues his third album 'The Urge' on the Relativity label. Following in the footsteps of 'Radio Free Albumuth' (1988 – Food For Thought Records) and 'Kings Of Sleep' (1989 – again Food For Thought), this is essentially a fusion instrumental album from the man who had made his name, as previously stated, with Joe Satriani. The reason this is of interest to Mötley fans is that Tommy is asked to guest on the title track.

'The Urge' is an album that sees Hamm going in an altogether rockier direction than previously, hence his decision to call upon the services of the Mötley skinbasher. Also featured on this album are guitarists Harry K. Cody and Eric Johnson.

The fact that such a 'musician's musician' as Hamm would ask Lee to play on his record speaks volumes for the way in which the latter had progressed as a drummer – also the respect he could command within the rock community. It's all too easy to forget Tommy's talent when confronted by his larger-than-life personality.

In July, Alice Cooper puts out his latest album, 'Hey, Stoopid!'. Produced by the formidable Peter Collins, it sees Alice bringing in a number of major guest musicians, including then-Judas Priest vocalist Rob Halford, Guns N'Roses

103

guitarist Slash, Ozzy Osbourne, guitar virtuosos Steve Vai and Joe Satriani, plus legendary actor Christopher Lee. Joining this distinguished throng are Mick Mars and Nikki Sixx, who co-wrote the song 'Die For You' with Alice and Canadian composer Jim Vallance. And Mick Mars' recognisable guitar signatures are present all over the tune.

All of this extra-curricular activity has one absentee: Vince Neil. Of course, he has been active over the past couple of years in the acting fraternity, appearing in the films *Police Academy VI* and *The Adventures Of Ford Fairlane*. Talking of his part in the latter as a 'dumb' rock'n'roller, Vince says:
"Yeah, that role was stupid, but it was kinda fun. I suppose a lot of people do think that's what I am, but I don't give a shit what people do or say."
But what has Neil been doing during this lull in the band's progress?
"I've been workin' out a lot. I'm really diggin' it too, fuckin' pumpin'... I've got a trainer and all that shit."

Neil also reveals during this interview with *Kerrang!* just how he missed touring...

"I would get bored when I first came off tour, because I love being on the road... I've stayed in the hotels when I come off the road just to feel that touring vibe. It's cool, y'get room service and, dunno, just the vibe of being on tour again... I know it's gonna stop one day, but when I retire I'm just gonna move to some island and live like a bum."

Before all of that, Vince has to drag himself back to reality when Mötley are confirmed to appear at the 11th annual Castle Donington Monsters Of Rock Festival, to be held on Saturday, August 17. The Crüe are third on the bill, surprisingly low considering their general stature in the rock world.

Topping the bill are Aussie legends AC/DC. It's their third headlining performance. Ironically, on their second appearance at Donington in 1984, Mötley had of course opened proceedings. Preceding AC/DC on the bill, and immediately above Mötley, would be Metallica, making their third appearance at the festival as well (they had been there in 1985 and 1987). Below Mötley are fast-rising blues-rockers the Black Crowes and Seattle's Queensrÿche, often referred to as the thinking man's metal band.

It is indeed an impressive bill. All of the acts had platinum albums in the US – the only time it had ever happened at Donington. Whilst it might be a little extreme to suggest that any, or all, of them could have headlined this festival, Metallica and Mötley certainly could have done so, whilst the other two acts are probably capable of being a lot higher up the bill than they are. Many feel that this was the strongest Donington line-up assembled since 1984 – and the show itself was to underscore such confidence.

The capacity at the Leicestershire site is, by this time, restricted to 72,500. This had been imposed in 1990, following the tragic deaths of two fans during Guns N'Roses' set two years earlier. The local council, as a result, had refused to grant a licence to local promoters MCP for the festival in 1989, and had only agreed to allow its return in 1990 (when Whitesnake were the headliners) on the condition that a crowd limit was imposed; previously the site of the festival could be expanded or contracted at will to accommodate the numbers.

Inevitably, given the strength and popularity of the bands on the bill in '91, tickets sell out very quickly, ensuring that the atmosphere on the day would be of the highest order. Expectations are very high – and the bands do not disappoint.

Three days prior to Donington, Mötley decide to play an unannounced club date at the Marquee Club in London. A tradition had by this time grown up whereby certain bands appearing on the Donington bill would play club shows either immediately prior to, or just after the festival itself. In 1987, Metallica had started it all off by performing at the 100 Club in central London. A year later, headliners Iron Maiden had taken up the baton and showed up at the Queen Mary College, London, whilst second on the bill Kiss played at The Marquee. In 1990, Donington special guests Aerosmith had followed up their triumphant Donington display with a Marquee date, during which Jimmy Page had joined them onstage. Now it's Mötley's turn to hit The Marquee's well-worn boards. Thus, just prior to Donington, a press release is sent out mysteriously announcing that The Fourskins, 'an unannounced, unrehearsed, unprofessional and ungodly-loud band' would be performing for the public's delectation at The Marquee on August 14. It doesn't take anyone with any gumption very long to figure out that this was Mötley. They had played in LA previously under such a moniker. Besides, such is the tradition with this type of show that bands enjoy word getting around about just who it is behind the pseudonym. Nothing inflates the egos of musicians as queues around the block and into the street, with fans being turned away.

Thus, the night itself arrives with a welter of sweaty bodies desperately trying to gain entrance into the small confines of The Marquee. Tickets outside are exchanging hands for upwards of ten times their face value, such is the desperation to gain entry to this most exclusive of gigs. When you consider that Mötley had played two sold-out dates at Wembley Arena the last time they were in London (at the end of 1989), one can readily understand the melée. Wembley holds some 10,000 fans. The Marquee holds less than 1000.

Mötley's performance that night is as sweaty and red hot as the heaving bodies pressed up against the stage. They even take time out to introduce a new number titled 'Primal Scream', which will appear on the 'Decade Of Decadence' album, and also play their version of the Sex Pistols' classic 'Anarchy In The UK', again a track they will include on 'Decade...'. It's the perfect warm-up for Donington and shows the waiting media and public alike that they will be one of the success stories on August 17.

So, the big day dawns, bringing with it tens of thousands of metalheads descending on the fields of Donington for their annual pilgrimage. And early in the afternoon, the Black Crowes take to the huge stage, ready to get proceedings rolling – except that they aren't exactly the right type of band for the festival. The Crowes' rock'n'roll anxieties aren't what the Donington crowd had been used to over the years, and an early rain shower does nothing to help the situation. Neil Jeffries, reviewing the band in *Kerrang!*, admitted that: "The Black Crowes are brilliant, but today they're misguided and misplaced. I find myself looking at my watch, hungry for Mötley Crüe and some mindless heavy metal". A back-handed compliment maybe, but one that showed where his sensibilities lay on the day. And he wasn't alone. Everyone, it seems, is waiting for da Crüe!

Next up come Queensrÿche, a classy metal band with a genuine streak of popularity among the huge crowd out front. They open with 'Revolution Calling' from the acclaimed 'Operation: Mindcrime' album and don't really look back. Admittedly, here is a band who are more at home amidst the dark intimacy of a theatre, but even in bright sunshine their quality breaks through. From then on, they pull the best cuts from their extensive repertoire, delighting the vast majority of the crowd.

And so to Mötley. This, as far as many are concerned, is the day's true highlight. The band are at their most explosive, detonating vast storehouses of musical dynamite as soon as they launch into opening track 'Kickstart My Heart', a truly memorable exposition of classic Crüe. This is quickly followed by 'Wild Side', as the band settle into their deadliest groove. Even the whipping wind cannot put the quartet off their considerable stride, the music coming through loud and bombastic. This is what Donington is all about.

Vince is in his most animated form as he roars out the greeting "Awlriiiighhhht Dooooningtooooon!" before the Crüe dive head-first into an awesome, fired-up version of 'Shout At The Devil'. From this point there's no stopping them as 'Live Wire', 'Piece Of Your Action', 'Primal Scream', 'Girls, Girls, Girls', 'Red Hot' and 'Dr. Feelgood' hit the spot and cascade down the spine. Finally, 'Anarchy In The UK' – Crüe customised, naturally – brings the curtain crashing down on a master performance. Simply magnificent is the general viewpoint. Who could tell from such a distance that this would be the last time the UK would bear witness to this incarnation of Mötley Crüe onstage? But what a way to go!

Metallica have the unenviable task of following Mötley, but their expert brand of extreme yet commercially aware metal proves equal to the task. These thrash heroes have the confidence, style and repertoire to ensure that they are not made to look foolish by the Crüe. But, even so, there is little doubt in most people's minds that Metallica are not quite as sharp and focused as Mötley had been.

Now, it's often said that Donington is tailor-made for the headlining act. They have the advantage of the intimacy provided by darkness within which to weave their magic, not to mention full use of the sound system and the lighting/special effects facilities. Thus, nobody ever steals the festival from the bill toppers, despite rumours to the contrary over the years. And so it proves today. AC/DC, with their vast experience and self-belief, rolled out yet another tried and trusted performance, pulling out all the tricks (the hanging bell, the cannons, Angus' school uniform, etc.) to ensure that when the reports are filed by journalists on the day's events their name would still be proudly right to the fore.

But, setting aside all the advantages enjoyed by AC/DC, it seems as if Mötley had been the band of the day according to most fans. They had apparently captured the intoxicating – not to mention intoxicated – atmosphere and heady bonhomie better than anyone during their display. A triumph – and a great way to say goodbye to the British public – at least in this present form.

A couple of days after Donington, Nikki goes shopping in London's Camden district and, "I heard this really shitty version of 'Primal Scream'. I looked round and I spotted this guy selling tapes of the *(Marquee)* gig! He saw me and was scared shitless 'cos he thought I was gonna jump him or something, but all I asked for was four copies! I love bootlegs. I'm a bootleg freak. It's a collectors' thing. It's not about the sound."

And if the proliferation of bootleg tapes is directly proportional to the popularity of the band in question, then Nikki had nothing to worry about at this juncture in Mötley's career. For, there are innumerable tapes of the band's Marquee and Donington shows floating around.

Two months after the Donington sensation, Mötley Crüe finally release the long-awaited 'Decade Of Decadence' album. It enters the Billboard charts in America at Number Two, only kept off the top spot by Guns N'Roses – not bad for what is essentially a collection of previously available material!

Amazing to think it's been ten long years since these four men tottered on their stiletto-heeled boots out of a cheap apartment off Sunset Boulevard and into heavy metal history. A decade on and LA, MTV and the whole metal scene are full of hairsprayed bands looking like leathered cherub junkies. But the Crüe have moved on and spearheaded what's to become another big rock bandwagon: sobriety. 'Decade Of Decadence' is a title that could get them arrested under the Trades Descriptions Act, what with the last two of their ten year history spent sober, straight, domesticated, anything but decadent. So much has changed since those early wacky and wacked-out days in Hollywood. All four members are now married, and Nikki is a father. Domestic bliss and fatherhood must have made some difference to the Mötley way of life.

"I haven't got a kid, so I don't know," Tommy tells Sylvie. "You don't call up and say, 'Nikki, let's get together' and he says, 'I've got to change the baby'. In that respect, us being friends, no it's never like that. He just brings little Gunnar along, and he has a nanny who takes care of the baby too, so it's not like he's got a ball and chain.

"You know, since I've been off the road I haven't been totally straight, I've gone out and gotten really fucked-up and it reminds me of the old days. But it's like, here I am doing the same old shit that I used to. This is boring! How many more years can I get fucked-up? There's got to be something else out there for me, and I'm always searching for it. You don't just find it overnight. You know, it took you ten years to learn how to get really fucking loaded and do your thing, and you're not going to find a new thing that makes you that happy overnight!" But it's the wrecked-and-wasted Crüe classics like 'Live Wire' and 'Piece Of Your Action' that start the album off, as the songs move in chronological order through the band's career – taking in their cover of Tommy Bolin's 'Teaser' on the 'Stairway To Heaven/Highway To Hell' compilation album and 'Rock'N'Roll Junkie' from *The Adventures Of Ford Fairlane* movie soundtrack on the way – right up to 'Kickstart My Heart', the musical testament to the event that nearly ended the band's career: Nikki Sixx's overdose; the injection of adrenalin to the heart that the paramedics gave him which brought him back after he'd been clinically declared dead.

The new stuff isn't, as you might expect, left-overs from the prolific 'Dr. Feelgood' sessions but brand new songs: 'Angela' and 'Primal Scream', and their cover of the Sex Pistols' 'Anarchy In The UK'. They were thinking of saving them for the next studio album, but the new stuff they've been writing, Tommy says, is even better.

"I think we're on kind of a roll. And no matter what we put on this record, there's so much new stuff, a whole lot of good material that's about to come out that we're not worried. There's plenty more where that came from!"
Talking at the time, Vince gives his definition of decadence:

"It's a state of mind. I was sittin' there havin' a drink at the Rainbow *(infamous LA night spot)* or somethin' and this guy comes up and starts telling me I'm not so wild or decadent and all this stuff. Thinking, I suppose, that I'd be all rowdy and stuff. And I just told him, 'Y'know why I'm not like that? It's because I don't have to be. I already am a pretty decadent person anyway'... The unexpected is decadent, the guy who's fucking straight-laced and you find out that he's fucking dogs or something."

During the same interview, Nikki looks back at the ten-year span of the Mötleys and makes some insightful points:

"The band is unpredictable. We never do what we're meant to, really. The stance with the JD bottle has been traded in for something we think is more rebellious. We may get that stance back, but who knows? We just find 'predictable' very boring and we really aren't sure what we're gonna do.

"We don't take anything seriously, which is probably the best part of the band... Some bands don't stir controversy, whereas Mötley Crüe seem to push some people's buttons... I don't know why people get hairs up their asses about us. Axl seems to have a hair up his ass about us. He slags us, so we slag him... If we actually met face to face, we'd just sit down, talk about it and say, 'Hey, this is stupid!'."

In November, a month after 'Decade...' appears, the Electric Love Hogs issue their eponymous debut album through London Records. Er, so what? Well, this record marks Tommy's debut as a producer. He handled production duties on two cuts, namely 'Sittin' Pretty' and 'Just Another Day', for the talented Americans, wacked-out funk-rockers in the Faith No More/Red Hot Chili Peppers style.

"I love what they do," enthuses Tommy. "That sorta music appeals to me at the moment. It was a ball workin' with them. I really wanna get more into producing, y'know."

The Electric Love Hogs themselves also shed some light on their reason for using Tommy:

"He'd wanted to produce a band for a long time," vocalist John Feldman states, "And all he ever got approached by were bands that were like Mötley Crüe. But he was lookin' for somethin' else." And there are even fans of the Crüe within the Hogs ranks. For instance, bassist Kelly LeMieux, who says "I was brought up on Mötley Crüe". In fact, the ELH actually play 'Shout At The Devil' regularly in their live set. And Tommy joins them onstage at The Roxy in LA one night to jam during this song.

So, a satisfying end to a satisfactory year. But what of the Crüe in '92? There is still, irritatingly, no sign of a new studio album, as designated producer Bob Rock continues to be held up by prior commitments. However, rehearsals have begun for this new record.

At one point, the Crüe actually think seriously about taking a radical departure with the next album by using more than one producer, as Tommy explains: "You know what? On this next record we've got, I don't know if you'll call it permission, but we've been allowed now space for 15, 16 songs, so we're probably going to spread our wings a little bit and write something a little 'outside'. There'll probably be an instrumental piece on there, something different. Not ten songs where you've got to have a format on it... On the next studio album we're actually thinking about getting Andy Johns to do two tracks, Bob Rock to do two. I don't know, pick a good producer... go out and have a different vibe from track to track...

That could be the album from hell that takes like eight years to make because no-one's fucking available!"

This could have as much to do with impatience as a desire to boldly go where etc etc. The drummer was sticking pins into voodoo dolls of Metallica when 'Decade...' was being held up as Bob Rock finished work on the Metallica album before producing the three new Crüe tracks.

It didn't quite turn out that way, but there are a few twists and turns to come before the next Crüe album hits the streets.

Just before the end of 1991, Tommy is quoted in American magazine *Circus* as saying: "If one member were to leave or die this would be the only Mötley Crüe that ever was."

Within a couple of months that quote would come back to haunt the drummer as 1992 makes its appearance.

Chapter Eleven – Without You

Well, the year 1992 begins confidently enough for Mötley, anyway. In January, the single 'Home Sweet Home ('91 Remix)' enters the UK charts at a promising position of Number 27. And that same month, Tommy swaps his drum sticks for a baseball bat as he participates in the third annual MTV 'Rock 'N' Jock' softball game in California. Not only does this slugfest provide enormous entertainment (and cheap television), but it also raises much-needed cash for the charitable TJ Martell Foundation, dedicated to providing money to help fight leukemia.
But the storm clouds are gathering – and are about to burst...

On February 10, Vince Neil turns up for rehearsal on the new album – only to be fired! Four days later, the band issue a statement explaining their sensational decision:

"Race car driving has become a priority in Neil's life, and he's dedicated much of his time and energy to it. The Crüe's relationship with Neil began to deteriorate because his bandmates felt he didn't share their determination and passion for music. Neil was the only Crüe member who didn't regularly participate in the songwriting process."

Nikki is quoted as saying: "After 11 years together, we've parted ways. I hope it can be as friendly and peaceful as possible, though in this business that sometimes is a difficult proposition."

How true that final thought is to prove. This is not going to be an amicable parting of the ways.

Vince, for his part, isn't slow in putting his case to the public via a press statement:

"I want to clear up some rumours about Mötley Crüe's break-up. I wasn't fired for drinking, and I didn't leave the band to pursue auto-racing, although that's been a hobby of mine for the past seven years. But it's never interfered with Mötley Crüe. Music has always been the top priority in my life.

"It is true, however, that I didn't share the enthusiasm for the band's new musical direction. When we started rehearsals, the music was heavier, the way Mötley Crüe used to be. When they brought in keyboards and more back-up singers, I was disappointed. But when I didn't agree with what they were doing, I was always shot down. I was the odd man out."

So, what really did happen? Did Mötley fire him for his outside activities, or was this just a convenient excuse? Were Mötley radically altering their musical direction?

Scarcely had the band issued their statement than Elektra were quick to point out that the reference to Vince's preoccupation with motor racing was not to be taken too seriously and was made half-jokingly. It seems strange that such an important press release should contain a thinly-veiled joke (as is claimed) that would be lost on everyone! Maybe, upon taking legal advice, Mötley and Elektra knew that such a statement could not be substantiated in any future action taken by Vince through the courts. Certainly, evidence suggests that Neil had a passion for motor racing, but no-one (either officially or otherwise) has ever hinted that this was out of control and endangering the delicate balance of, and prospects for, the Crüe.

So, what of Vince's assertions about the state of Mötley's music? That certainly rings true. Tommy has already openly stated his fascination with the new styles coming through into rock music via grunge, funk-metal, etc. His work with the Electric Love Hogs showed where his musical heart currently lay. And Nikki has always had a keen ear for musical development and change. It seems clear that these two at least know that if the Crüe are to survive then they must adapt and mature. It is no use standing still. Vince, on the other hand, is far more conservative.

However, this alone would not account for the decision to remove a crucial part of the band. And it would seem logical that, although, to the public at large, everything is hunky-dory between the various Crüesters, nonetheless there had been a gradual rift developing between Neil on the one hand and the remaining three on the other. Perhaps his central role in the growing chasm between Mötley and Guns N'Roses plays its part. Perhaps there are other reasons, equally as important. Whatever, the icing on the cake is probably provided by the musical arguments, at which point any slight irritation Neil was causing the band (such as his motor racing interest) might well assume virtual apocalyptic proportions.

But this is not to be a smooth split. By October, Neil has issued a law suit against the band, seeking $5 million in damages, 25 per cent of all profits made by Mötley on future albums and, just to rub salt in the wounds, reinstatement in the Crüe! Part of this claim is based on the fact that just prior to this incident, Mötley had signed a new $25 million deal with Elektra, with the singer very much an equal partner in this contract. Thus, although he is no longer a member of the band, legally Neil claims rights to a quarter of all profits made by the Mötley organisation on every album released under the terms of this deal!

Indeed, it's even whispered in certain quarters that Mötley had deliberately delayed making the decision to get rid of Vince, because they wanted the contract with Elektra signed, sealed and delivered first. If word had got out that Neil was no longer to be a part of the band, then it was felt that this could jeopardise the entire deal.

If Nikki had really hoped for a convivial, friendly understanding between the parties concerned, he is to be bitterly disappointed.

Mötley lose no time in trying to replace Vince, but it is to prove a difficult and lengthy process. All four members of the band have their own distinct personality. They are all equally as recognisable to fans. This was certainly not a case of getting rid of a backroom boy. Not since David Lee Roth had quit Van Halen in 1985 had a band been faced with such a difficult personnel task. Van Halen chose to solve their problem by going for another personality in Sammy Hagar, yet one who was radically different to his predecessor. Mötley seem to be uncertain as to exactly who, or what, they wanted.

Immediately nominated as favourite for the job is The Scream vocalist John Corabi – his band being widely tipped for big things within the music industry. However, Stephen Shareaux (from LA band Kik Tracee) and Marq Torien of the disintegrating BulletBoys are also mentioned in despatches. Indeed, reports emanating from LA claim that Mötley audition Shareaux in March, a similar type of singer to Neil, but decide he's not what they're looking for.

More fancifully, David Lee Roth's name is linked with the job, and even Stephen Pearcy, one-time frontman for the defunct Ratt and an old friend of Mötley's, gets his name into the ever-widening frame. But within weeks of Neil's departure, Corabi is the one remaining name being bandied about in knowing circles. It seems just a matter of time before he is confirmed.

Whilst all this is going on, Mötley are keeping a low profile – a very low profile, anxious to cement their new line-up before making public pronouncements. Neil, though, isn't slow to get off the mark and hit out at his erstwhile colleagues. At the time he had put out his original statement, the singer had said, "I'm going to start recording in the next couple of months. All my rock buddies have been really supportive and want to help on the record. I'm really excited about it". Now he puts his plans into practice.

Shortly after his sacking, the Disney organisation call him, not to offer the blond a part in the re-make of *Bambi*, but to ask him to record a song for the forthcoming movie titled *Encino Man*. The film (which is to be released in the UK as *California Man*) is a typical '90s youth-oriented affair, starring hot young crazy comedian Pauly Shore, who had rocketted to fame via MTV in the States. Neil accepts the offer and gets together with old pals Jack Blades (bassist – once of Night Ranger) and Tommy Shaw (guitarist – previously with Styx), both of whom are now with platinum act Damn Yankees.

The song in question, 'You're Invited, But Your Friend Can't Come', takes the trio just 20 minutes to write, being a mild-mannered dumbo hard rock anthem that wouldn't challenge the braincell, but is nevertheless entertaining in a retro way.

"The whole thing came together at the right time," Neil says, "because after all the rumours, and that first press release came out saying that I'd quit... y'know people tend to believe the first thing that they read. And I wanted people to know that I didn't give up rock'n'roll."

Neil also too time out to scotch the stories spreading about his excessive drinking habits being behind his eventual dismissal...

"Fuckin' three-quarters of Mötley Crüe were drinking, and most of 'em were going out every night fuckin' partying. I wasn't any worse or any better than anyone else in the band.

"I really don't know about this I'm not rock'n'roll enough thing (mentioned by the Crüe), because maybe I'm too rock'n'roll for them now. I wanna stay with the Mötley tradition of rocking. We were a great rock'n'roll band and it just isn't that anymore, because they had nothing else to blame... Basically, what broke the band up was Nikki's ego, because I really wasn't that happy with the music... At the time when I was rehearsing, his vision was to write another 'Physical Graffiti'. But the songs were sounding like fourth-rate songs from 'Physical Graffiti'."

Furthermore, the singer scoffs openly about the claims being made concerning his motor racing commitments...

"I was always at rehearsal. I was always the first one to rehearsal. I was always doing my job. I was at rehearsal every day, so what time was it taking up? "I showed up for rehearsal one day and went into the studio room and I go, 'Where is everybody?' to one of the crew guys. So he told me, 'Oh, they're upstairs'. So I went upstairs and the band are sitting there with our manager, so I knew something was gonna happen."

The blond frontman claims that, at this point, Nikki told him that the Crüe were considering getting a new singer, because of differences in musical outlook between Neil and the others.

"This was absolutely the biggest surprise I've ever had in my life! I didn't have an inkling that this was gonna happen. I mean, I wouldn't have driven an hour in the rain to go to rehearsal to get fired... That the band did this told me that they were never really my friends in the first place... I thought Mötley were my friends for the last 11 years and if they were gonna fire me they at least could've done it in a different way. Before you fire someone, don't you a least talk to them and go, 'This ain't workin' any more'?

"I was gonna keep it really mellow *(after the departure)* and then Nikki went ahead and put out his own press release on the band's behalf, saying all this bullshit, and as soon as I read that, I was like, 'Well, fuck them, man! I want people to really know what happened!'."

Neil also insists that there is no possibility of a reunion. Not surprising, really, given the bad blood at the time.

Vince now signs a solo deal with Warner Brothers and prepares to record his own album; the single 'You're Invited, But Your Friend Can't Come' sees the light of day on the Disney subsidiary Hollywood Records in May and is a minor hit in both the UK and US.

The singer enters the studio in August with veteran producer Ron Nevison, having recruited a strong band around him. Joining Vince on this project are former Ozzy Osbourne/Beggars & Thieves bassist Phil Soussan, guitarists Robbie Crane and Steve Stevens (the latter most associated with Billy Idol) and drummer Vikki James Foxx (previously with Enuff Z'Nuff).

The much-respected Stevens virtually becomes Neil's musical partner. Indeed, the singer says that the diminutive guitarist is top of his hit list when assembling the band:

"Billy Idol actually called me right after it *(the Mötley departure)* happened and said he would get hold of Steve for me, and he did."

Stevens leaves the ill-fated Jerusalem Slim, within which he was, ironically, working with former Hanoi Rocks singer Michael Monroe; once again Neil is unwittingly responsible for splitting up one of Monroe's bands. In 1984, following the car crash that killed Razzle, Hanoi call it a day. Now it's the turn of Jerusalem Slim.

Recalling this fact, Monroe himself shows little disappointment at losing Stevens to Neil, when Sylvie questions him about this in 1994...

"It's ironic. That right there tells you why it didn't work out *(in Jerusalem Slim)*. Shit, I don't wanna talk about that guy *(Stevens)*. I'm not bitter *(about Vince breaking up a second band)*. I'm just saying good riddance! I'm thankful to Vince Neil for doing me a favour, for helping me get rid of that guy."
The remaining three members of Vince's band are carefully screened before being recruited. Thus, the Vince Neil Band (or VNB for short) is ready for action.

They finally go into the studio with Nevison, with the singer determined that his personal musical ideals and outlook will be reflected in the final product. "It's rock'n'roll in the Mötley vein... but like a '90s version of Mötley Crüe maybe... it's more advanced and a lot more musical."

The original intention for VNB is to
release their album on February 10, 1993,
the first anniversary of their singer's
split with Mötley.

"It's something that I can really shoot
for," Vince tells *Kerrang!* at the back end of
'92. "I just think it would be kinda like a
big, 'Hey, screw you, look at this – one year
later I've got a new record out!'."

Vince seems to be finding the fresh challenge
very stimulating, especially working with new
faces.

"I am kinda set in my ways, but I'm learning to
go beyond that... it's good for me. I'm getting to be
more creative... I don't wanna step backwards. I
wanna take it from where I was and just keep going –
that's what I'm shooting for... Everybody takes this stuff
too seriously these days. Loosen up, man – it's only
rock'n'roll!"

But the recording process for this new album isn't to be without its
hiccups. For the second time in a matter of months Vince is to be
embroiled in a personality clash – except this time he's on the other
side of the fence.

Soussan leaves the VNB whilst they're still putting the album together,
accusing Neil and Stevens of dominating the rest of the band and
imposing their idea without discussion. How strange. Neil, though,
dismisses Soussan's claim, and with time running out Crane switches
from rhythm guitar to play all the bass lines on the album.
Dave Marshall (previously with LA singer Fiona) is brought
in to play rhythm guitar.

Meantime, back in the Crüe quarters, Corabi is the only name
now being mentioned for Neil's position. Every other candidate
seems to have been permanently eliminated from the race,
including Shareaux, who issues his own statement on what
happened between him and the band:
"I've always loved the Crüe and the fact that they were
interested in me joining the band has made this one of the biggest
events in my life. But we've mutually agreed that musically it
didn't feel right for either of us. I'm proud of what I've
established in my heart, and in my art, with Kik Tracee, and
I've nothing but the deepest respect for Mötley Crüe."

With Corabi writing and working on material with the Crüe boys by mid-July, why wasn't anybody confirming his recruitment? Two reasons spring to mind: Firstly, the three founder-members of Mötley wanted to be absolutely certain that this was really the guy for them. They could not afford to make any mistakes in public.

Secondly, Corabi is contractually tied to Hollywood Records through The Scream. Before anything could be announced, everything needed to be agreed legally between Mötley Crüe, Elektra, The Scream and Hollywood. Not as easy as it would seem.

A year later, when asked how they found Corabi, Nikki tells Sylvie:

"*Rolling Stone* had asked me my ten favourite albums or something, and The Scream album *('Let It Scream')* was one of the albums I had bought and was listening to over and over. And John called the office. He wanted to thank me for mentioning the band's name. And it was right at the same time that everything happened with Vince. So, I got his phone number and called him. I said, 'Hi, this is Nikki from Mötley, do you want to come down and audition for the band?'. He was kind of freaked out. 'What are you talking about?'. I said, 'Come down and we'll tell you'. And that's how it happened. I tell you, I'm a happy motherfucker."

Corabi himself recalls how, when he first read the *Rolling Stone* story, he wondered whether Nikki was actually referring to his band at all.
"There used to be a punk band out of Washington DC also called The Scream."
The singer's first steps with Mötley are rather tentative.

"I wasn't real familiar with a lot of their material. We just jammed on some of the covers that they'd done on their records, like 'Helter Skelter', 'Jailhouse Rock', and I think I learned 'Dr. Feelgood'. And it was real cool. The guys, contrary to popular belief, are probably the nicest people you ever want to meet. They're really nice, really down to earth, they just treat everybody really cool."

By the Summer of '92 Mötley, with Corabi seemingly in place, are in the studio with producer Bob Rock. The plan is apparently to have the album finished by the end of '92, ready to match Vince with the release of their record. However, as Christmas approaches, rumours begin to circulate that Mötley have finished the record (tentatively titled 'Til Death Do Us Part'), and delivered it to Elektra... who promptly reject it as not being good enough!

Nikki vehemently denies this story:

"There was no plan to release it at the same time as Vince's album... I didn't sign the record contract with Elektra so that I could be rushed. There was only one reason I signed it and that was to make records the way I wanted. That meant if I want to spend a year in the studio – and this album is going to end up taking a solid year of studio work and we were locked in the room writing music for eight to 11 months before that – then that's what I do...

"We had kind of hoped to get our album out by this October *(1993)*, then Bob Rock got an offer to play with Bon Jovi in Europe with his band Rockhead and he asked us if we minded. We had about 14 songs ready then, and we had what everybody believed was a better album than 'Dr. Feelgood' by 100 per cent. But we said, 'Go ahead, and we'll just go and rehearse and maybe a couple more ideas will come up'. And we ended up with almost a whole other album of material – nine or ten new songs."

But other informed sources suggest that part of the reason Bob Rock takes the offer from old pals Bon Jovi is precisely because he feels that Mötley's album still needs work in the songwriting department before they go back into the studio. Malcolm Dome does know that Mötley are sending out tapes to Rock whilst the latter is in Europe, so that he can ascertain whether what they are coming up with is of an acceptable standard.

By the end of the year, there is some better news for the Crüe, in the form of 'Crüeball', a new video pinball game, designed by Electronic Arts for the Sega Genesis system and featuring three Mötley tracks within the format of the game itself.

Meantime, Mick takes advantage of the fact that the band still have some time on their hands by helping his wife to put together her own band, Alice In Thunderland, although nothing is to come of this exercise.

Vince ends the year in a somewhat more ludicrous fashion. He purchases the licensing rights for the 'Hawaiian Tropic' range of beach swimwear. He adds this acquisition to another range of swimwear called 'Xposure' that he already owns, designs and distributes in partnership with his wife. Ah well, something to fall back on if the solo career flops.

Chapter Twelve
A New Beginning

Although Mötley are still making no official pronouncement to the waiting world, by early 1993 it seems as if any problems connected with the recruitment of John Corabi have been cleared up.

Word in the music industry has it that the sticking point all along had actually been Corabi's contractual ties with Hollywood Records. The latter are reputed to want a payment in excess of $1 million to let him walk free from The Scream. Mötley are unwilling to play such a vast and inflated sum.

Eventually, a satisfactory compromise is agreed, whereby Corabi would be allowed to leave The Scream and join Mötley, but would also be obliged to record a solo album for Hollywood at an undisclosed point in the future. Nobody loses face.

How ironic, though, that Hollywood Records should have ended up playing such a major role in the Mötley upheaval. They are the company who offer Vince a quick way back into action via the soundtrack for *California Man*. Now, they are the ones apparently blocking his successor taking up the reins – albeit temporarily. Walt Disney would probably be turning in his grave if he could see his beloved organisation involved with the less than squeaky clean world of Mötley Crüe!

But, who is this fella John Corabi, anyway?

Born in Philadelphia, he started off playing guitar on the Philly and South Jersey scene, working with various local covers bands.

"I'd play four sets a night doing Journey and mellow stuff. To give the singer a break, I'd do Van Halen, Led Zeppelin, Aerosmith."

Moving to LA – where all budding musos tended to end up in the late '80s – Corabi eventually teamed up with bassist John Alderete and guitarist Bruce Bouillet in the final incarnation of local heroes Racer X (most known back then for giving guitarist Paul Gilbert lift-off towards fame in Mr Big). He joined this act from failed Californian band Angora. But Racer X were only to last a couple more months before drummer Scott Travis quit to replace Dave Holland in Judas Priest.

Undeterred, Corabi (now concentrating solely on his singing), Bouillet and Alderete found skinsman Walt Woodman III (who had previously been with Americade) – and The Scream were born, although they originally chose to call themselves Saints And Sinners. Signing a deal with Hollywood Records led the foursome into working with legendary producer Eddie Kramer on their debut album, 'Let It Scream'. This was released to much critical acclaim in 1991.

However, despite the approval of rock magazines everywhere, the record failed to set the cash registers going and didn't gain the expected commercial success. Thus, when Nikki made his watershed remarks about The Scream to *Rolling Stone* and Corabi phoned him, the die was cast. Interestingly enough, Mötley weren't the first name band to approach Corabi. Both Britny Fox and Skid Row had previously made unsuccessful offers for his services, the latter prior to Sebastian Bach being recruited.

Certainly, the Mötleys seem delighted with their choice when they speak about Corabi.

Nikki: "He plays guitar and he plays harmonica and he writes and he's got an amazing voice. And he totally fits in with us visually: all tattoos and black hair – we don't need blonds anyway, do we? But we got John because of his talent, not because of the way he looked. We were just looking for someone that we felt we could click with. Because I don't intend doing this every ten years! It was something I was forced to do, and I don't plan on doing it again. So we wanted to be sure that it was somebody we wanted to spend time with, musically and personally.

"We hang out together. It's great. Yeah, he's the new guy in the band and we totally fuck with him all the time. But he's also somebody I can see myself playing in a band with for as long as I can see into the future."

Tommy (talking to an English rock magazine): "The thing about John is that I get to relive all this stuff *(the early days)*. We recently went to our tour manager's wedding, and we had a helicopter land at my house to pick us up and fly over to Catalina Island. Anyway, John's at my house and we're standing at my bar and he hears this thing and goes, 'What the fuck is going on?'. I go, 'We're going to hop in a helicopter and blaze over to the island'. And he's like, 'Fuck! No fucking way!'.

"Just to see his eyeballs pop out of his head, you know, and experience this stuff... How many times have we been in a helicopter, a bunch of us, and he's going, 'This is insane'. So we get to relive it around him. We get to laugh and watch him enjoy it as well... The dude is not green by any means musically, but as far as experiences go along the way, it's fun to watch him freak out.

25

"I can't even wait for the first show. I'll be laughing behind my drums the whole time. I'll toss him a few rolls of toilet paper so he can literally shit himself... There's no problem with filling Vince's shoes and beyond, so he has nothing to worry about in that department."

Mick (*Kerrang!*): "With John involved, it's given me more scope. I'd limit myself previously, with a view to how the material would be played live. Now, the pressure's off. The first time John came in and played guitar, I just went, 'Fuck!'. He's more melodic. He gave me a kick and you can tell on the record, 'cos I was able to go off into areas I could've done in the past but didn't."

There, that all makes sense, doesn't it?!

Nikki takes time out whilst in the throes of recording the album to give a few hints about what the world could expect from the new Mötley:
"There are no 'pussy' songs on the album, absolutely not one. Those songs were written by me for Vince – he always loved that kind of stuff, and I've always been a little more serious. It's just great music...

"We've worked with a couple of guys from *(Canadian avant-garde act)* Skinny Puppy on one song – they did some sequencing. We've got a 60-piece orchestra coming in tomorrow for a song we've got called 'Misunderstood' that's ten minutes long and everybody keeps saying is the next 'Stairway To Heaven'. There's a song called 'Miss Baby Kills' that has a sort of 'Dr. Feelgood' feel. It was called 'My Way Or The Highway' before, then Tommy was like, 'We don't have any 'Fuck' songs on this album!'. And I go, 'I hate those kind of lyrics'. And he goes, 'Well does it have to be fucking cheesy? Can't it be kind of cool?'. So, I had some Ian Hunter kind of lyrics about this girl who's real bad, and the chorus goes, *'I've seen flowers and razor blades in her hair/She's walking trouble with an innocence/She keeps me high/Miss Baby Kills!'*. It's a fun song... Everybody that hears the record fucking freaks!

"If they *(Mötley fans)* like great music, they're going to like it. The kids who like the more aggressive Mötley are going to really sink their teeth into this, because John is like a real aggressive singer. And when it's beautiful, it's even more heart-wrenching because he's such an amazing singer. He's a songwriter too, which we didn't have before. And together, me and John have written all the lyrics." (One can only wonder why Tommy seems intent to have a 'Fuck' song on the album, when according to Nikki, those songs in the past were written specifically for Vince!)

Whilst everybody in the Mötley camp is bending over backwards in their praise of John, when the subject of Vince raises its ugly head, darker thoughts emanate.

Nikki: "I haven't had any second thoughts *(about replacing Vince)*. From the day it happened I knew it was time to move on."

"The most important thing for me has always been the band. I need to make music. I need a vehicle to express myself. I don't care if I'm playing a club or playing a stadium – without music I don't have a fucking purpose. Music is everything for me – I dress it, I've shot it in my veins, everything. And I knew we were doing the right thing. Because I have a lot of faith in this band. There are some great players, great writers, great chemistry... everything.

"Have you ever been in a relationship with someone where you've just stuck with them and stuck with them and they just kept doing the same things, and finally it just wasn't worth it any more? That's exactly how it was. It just wasn't worth it any more. We kept seeing the same things and requesting the same things and getting the same reactions. It dissolved itself. It just didn't work any more. And I'm really fucking glad, because now I won't have a stomach ache any more. It was that bad.

"I would bust this fucking band up before we got back together *(with Vince)*. This is Mötley Crüe, take it or leave it. As it is, I refuse to go back. I only want to go forward. How could I be in a band with somebody who is this talented and go back? We're not going to slag the guy, because we're above that. We're not into playing high school games and stuff. We're into making music, not soap operas. Fuck it! Who cares anyway... we got somebody who's really fucking talented *(ie Corabi)*. We didn't just get anybody to do it for the money. We got somebody who is musically brilliant."

When Sylvie suggests to Nikki that some people do get back together, he replies:

"Uh-uh. I'm not like that. I've never called an old girlfriend."

Well, that's not strictly true. Nikki did talk to Lita Ford long after they'd split up, otherwise how did they co-write the song 'Falling In And Out Of Love'? But we get the point – Vince is the past, John is the present and the future. Meantime, as the Mötleys continue to work on their most important album since 'Too Fast For Love', Vince gets back in the saddle during April when he issues his long-awaited first post-Mötley album, 'Exposed' through Warner Brothers. It receives a lukewarm response from the media and fans alike. Neil's time-honoured brand of basic rock'n'roll is seemingly out of step with the current musical climate. Mind you, it begins its chart sojourn well enough in America, entering the Billboard Top 200 at Number 13. But it soon plummets, vanishing altogether after a matter of weeks. In the UK, things are even worse, the album charting at Number 44, before disappearing.

On the touring front, Vince makes it plain from the start exactly what he's looking to do:

"We're not playing any clubs. No theatres either. Actually, our first shows are gonna be stadiums, as part of a package later this year. From there, we'll go into

127

arenas. Why would I go into the clubs from arenas? Y'know what? I don't wanna go backwards, and I don't have to go backwards. For me, playing a club is going backwards.

"Look, Mötley Crüe were always about production, giving the kids a $50 show for a $20 ticket. That's what I wanna continue doing: rip people's faces off and give 'em a great show. I don't give a fuck what anybody else does. I saw the Chili Peppers and Nirvana at the *(LA)* Sports Arena and I counted 15 lights! I thought that was kinda bogus... Maybe I'm from the old school that thinks bigger is better. It's fun for me to see lasers shooting out and lights going everywhere and the stage doin' something weird. It's fun for everyone, players and audience... On tour I'll be exactly who I have been for the past ten years."

Bold words. And things do start off reasonably well for Vince and his cohorts as they're invited to support Van Halen on a huge arena/stadium tour of the US; it's even suggested that the VNB are paid a vast sum of money to do this opening slot, Van Halen believing that the former Mötley man would be a valuable added attraction on the bill. But after this finishes, things start to go wrong for Neil and his merry men. A proposed Summer '93 American tour with Coverdale-Page falls apart, when the latter elect not to go out on the road in the States, and with no sign of a replacement arena package in sight, Vince is forced to swallow his pride and go out to play smaller venues on his own, before the whole operation grinds to a halt early in '94 when throat problems necessitate the cancellation of all touring plans.

However, the headlining shows VNB do undertake in theatres get a reasonably good response – even if they're not attracting sell-out crowds. Vince gets an early taste of the dire problems Mötley are soon to face – not being able to sell anywhere near enough tickets to make the touring process economically viable. The set being played by VNB draws from the 'Exposed' album (numbers such as 'You're Invited, But Your Friend Can't Come', 'Look In Her Eyes', 'Can't Have Your Cake', 'Sister Of Pain' and 'Gettin' Harder'), but also includes such Mötley classics as 'Girls, Girls, Girls', 'Kickstart My Heart', 'Looks That Kill' and 'Dr. Feelgood'. They also throw in a cover of The Sweet's 'Set Me Free'. So, with Vince having beaten Mötley out of the box and found the reception rather chilly, attention now turns towards Nikki, Mick, Tommy and John as 1993 draws to a close. But the portents are not that good. The whole music scene has changed dramatically in the lengthy period since Mötley were last in action. And one does wonder whether they could get close to matching previous multi-platinum achievements.

At the beginning of 1994, Mötley gear up towards the imminent release of their new album, now retitled 'Motley Crue', by doing the usual round of interviews with the world's music media. During this stint, they speak openly of the new record (and the change in musical direction it is to herald) and also of their feelings towards Vince from a 'safe' distance of virtually two years.

128

129

Firstly, the music:

Nikki: "There were a couple of times where Tommy would complain that there was, 'No fun shit' on the record and I'd say, 'I'm not in a funny mood!'. He'd fire back, 'Well, other people like to have their fun!', and I'd say, 'Well, that's their fuckin' problem!'. I was real adamant that there would be no pussy songs on the album. I wrote those not for me, but for Vince...

"But, if you look back at our albums, they'd always been split down the middle. There would be the pussy stuff and then there would be the others with more of a serious touch to them... I just made this conscious decision not to do what we'd done on most of our albums. It was an easy transition 'cos it was what I always did better anyway... So, having 24 songs to write lyrics for with John, I had to home in on subjects. There was no escape valve. It involved more work, but it was far more satisfying.

"There was a lot of experimenting that went down that gave it this texture. It sounds real heavy at first, but by the sixth or seventh play you discover all this stuff way deep in the tracks that you really need headphones to discover at all... I wanted to make a great album. I don't know who is gonna like it. It's just a great album, that's all that matters."

Tommy: "I know we're gonna lose a lot of fans, but hopefully gain a lot more. There's a new generation out there and tastes change. To be brutally honest, all the new music has really inspired me. Some good bands have come through whilst we've been away."

Nikki: "Thank God that a lot of the crap from the '80s is gone. It was time that a lot of the garbage got cleared out so new things could come in. I'm not worried about the way Mötley Crüe will be accepted. I've always believed that people don't want to get into image or what you're wearing, they want to get into great music... We're in the midst of an important transition. We're not a party band any more.

"You always need some kind of anarchy in rock'n'roll to clear out the pipeline. The Sex Pistols did it in the '70s, we did it in the '80s, somebody else is doing it now.

"I like industrial and house music and stuff like that. I like Smashing Pumpkins (*presumably the band, not the activity!*), the new Iggy Pop album, Nirvana – but there aren't too many people who are moving me musically."

Nikki, whose first record purchase was Harry Nilsson's 'Nilsson Schmilsson' album(!), also admits to a liking for the Manic Street Preachers, Suede, Teenage Fanclub and Pantera. He even speaks about the possibility of doing some interesting covers on the next Mötley tour.

"I really want to go through our album collections and pull out a whole host of different things to play live... I mean, I love the Manic Street Preachers and I wouldn't mind doing one of their songs live. We might even do a Pantera song, too!"

On a more prosaic and down to earth note, Nikki explains why the album had changed title from 'Til Death Do Us Part' to 'Motley Crue'...

"We were going to call it 'Til Death...' – we had a song called that, and the title was pretty cool because it related to us and our fans and our tattoos and the new marriage of us and John. But the title had been around for so long that Bob Rock said, 'God, it feels like the album's already come and gone'. So, we were designing the album cover and I said, 'Hey, just for something different, let's take the title off'. And it was like, 'Fuck, that's cool!'."

As far as Vince Neil is concerned, Nikki pulls no punches:
"There was a rumour goin' around that I had this master plan and that even before 'Decade Of Decadence', I knew all along that we'd get rid of Vince Neil and that he was just used to sign a new label deal, after which we fired him. None of it's true.

"We never fired Vince – he walked out of the band. I think it was some form of martyrdom on his part. We call him 'The Victim' now, 'cos he's been telling everybody, 'Well, they fired me – woe is me!'.

"He wasn't fired. He was really unhappy with the music, unhappy with us pushing him to better himself and rise to the occasion. We were never happy settling on anything... We were always trying to better ourselves and I believe over the years it wore Vince down.

"Anything we've said about him has just been honest. Sometimes that honesty might seem like we're slagging him, but we're just stating what happened... It's better than just turning round saying, 'He's a fuckin' asshole', 'cos that's what he did to us. At least he could explain why we're assholes. We were assholes because we asked him to do things he didn't want to – like grow as a musician?"

Strange that Nikki now suggests Vince walked out all along. The first press release from the band in 1992 strongly hinted that he had been sacked, and every quote subsequently from Mötley affirmed that belief. Are the band now changing their story, or was that original statement misleading, an act of bravura?

Tommy also has things to say about Vince...

"None of us wish Vince any bad luck. If anything, we were all sad for the dude, because he didn't take the tools we showed him and do anything fucking good with them. He just went and did an average product. He didn't really take his time... But it's real nice to have a fourth member who's just as into the music as we are – if not more. Before, other things were more important than the music." Nikki: "A reunion with Vince Neil will not happen. There's not enough money in it to make it happen. I'd rather have a mediocre career as a solo artist or as a member of another band, having enjoyed the arena level already, and go on and enjoy being happy as a musician, than prostitute myself out."

Thus, with a reunion temporarily at least ruled out, 'Motley Crue' is released on March 14. Just prior to this, Elektra host a party for the band when they're in London to help launch the record (a similar party is to take place later in New York). It's at the Hard Rock Café. Among the guests who turn up are former Iron Maiden vocalist Bruce Dickinson, current Maiden guitarist Janick Gers, plus the three members of fast-rising Irish combo Therapy?. It's a fun evening, although John Corabi's leather jacket, complete with the name 'Motley Crue' emblazoned on the back in rather cheap script, causes a few guffaws, with certain amused onlookers wondering aloud whether Corabi carries the band's name on his back just so that he would remember which group he's actually joined!

Tommy turns up at this party in the company of his new girlfriend Bobbi Browne (not to be confused with the soul singer, this particular BB was previously married to Jani Lane, vocalist with Warrant). Lee's marriage to Heather Locklear is now effectively over, with divorce proceedings underway. The pair had split up towards the end of 1993.

"We never saw each other," Tommy says of the breakdown of his marriage. "I'd be working, either doing records or touring and she'd be on TV. They say absence makes the heart grow fonder, but man, too much absence makes it wander! When you don't see someone for a good while you begin to crave affection, sex, whatever, elsewhere."

After the split with Tommy, Heather starts dating Bon Jovi guitarist Richie Sambora. Given the still-strained relationship between Mötley and Bon Jovi, this is indeed ironic.

Tommy isn't alone in facing domestic upheavals. Mick is getting divorced from Emi Canyn, and John has also left his wife, Val. Only Nikki remains happily wrapped in marital bliss. And this Mötley nuptial turmoil has even affected Vince, who splits up with Sharise. For a short while, the singer is actually dating actress Shannen Doherty, star of the hit US TV series *Beverly Hills 90210*.

The album 'Motley Crue' enters the US charts at Number Seven, but suffers a similar fate to that of Vince's record – it doesn't hang around. The band also

incurs the wrath of Elektra when the original sleeve depicts Nikki in a Nazi uniform. The label orders half-a-million copies of the sleeve boasting this photograph to be destroyed and a second, altogether less controversial cover, replaces it. Nikki is not amused:

"It pisses me off. Don't ever tell me what to do and what not to do. But I'll have my own way, because our stage show will feature loads of mannequins, all dressed up in Nazi uniforms. And we're only doing that 'cos Elektra tried to dictate to us."

By contrast to this determination to incorporate some form of Germanic statement into their live show, Mötley actually elect at this stage to drop the famous umlauts over the 'o' of 'Mötley' and the 'u' of Crüe'. It is almost as if this is their way of saying goodbye to the past.

The bassist also has little sympathy with Elektra's disappointment over the relatively poor sales figures for the new record:

"The record company are probably having a heart attack. They wanted us to do six or seven million copies. But I told them that this is like 'Shout At The Devil' all over again. We have to go out and build it up again."

The British rock press, though, seems to be rather impressed with the album. Mike Peake of *Kerrang!* reckons, "The Crüe are still relevant. Don't ever let fashion deny you freedom of choice", whilst Dave Ling of *RAW* says, "For the most part 'Motley Crue' is like going ten rounds with Mike Tyson... It's not what people will expect and takes a little persevering with but, one or two inconsistencies aside, it remains a damn fine record".

Arguably the most amusing report on the LP comes in the prestigious daily the *New York Post*. "Anybody who steps in the for late Vince Neil (who died in a car accident)," they claim, "has major shoes to fill".

Ooops, talk about getting your facts ever so slightly confused!

The 'Motley Crue' album on first listen is a welcome breath of fresh air from the band. It is a huge departure from previous albums. Whereas there was a linear development in the Crüe from 'Too Fast For Love' through to 'Dr. Feelgood', this time they had taken off in an exponential direction. Certainly it draws heavily on the new music that was so dominant on the scene (grunge, industrial, house, etc.), but there are still the Mötley teethmarks buried deep in the musical flesh.

135

137

'Power To The Music' is aggressively bare-knuckled (Mötley in the raw), whilst 'Uncle Jack' is a little more esoteric, a little more daring, calling to mind Alice In Chains at their most profligate. The first single, 'Hooligan's Holiday' ("I guess it's about us," says Tommy) is vibrant, thundering along in momentous style. The accompanying video owes much to the classic movie *Clockwork Orange* and is directed by Nick Egan.

"The pussy channel *(MTV)* won't play it," roars Tommy. "They get upset when they see a nipple or even the shadow of a gun."

'Misunderstood' (featuring former Deep Purple great Glenn Hughes on backing vocals) has a weird, almost dreamy feel to it. Nikki describes it as being, "The Beatles' 'Strawberry Fields' meets Led Zeppelin". This song actually dates back to Vince's last days with the band; it is thought to be one of the reasons for the singer's departure. The acoustically delicate 'Loveshine' is followed by the melodic yet punky 'Poison Apples' ("I sort of wrote it talking about how I took a bus from Seattle to Idaho, and from Idaho to Hollywood to play rock'n'roll," says Nikki). The mid-paced 'Hammered' is one of the earliest tunes constructed by the band after Corabi's arrival, whilst 'Til Death Us Do Part' is cruelly metallic and noxious.

'Welcome To The Numb' lives up to Nikki's claim that this is "really up riff-wise, kind of like 'Draw The Line' from Aerosmith". 'Smoke In The Sky' is out-and-out metal mayhem and 'Droppin' Like Flies' again drifts back towards the sound and style of the darker side of grunge. Finally, the mellow 'Driftaway' brings proceedings to a halt on a ballady, yet certainly not a wimpy, note.

Early impressions on this album are positive in the extreme, but it dissolves all too easily. There is no real taste left on the palate, as is certainly the case with 'Too Fast For Love', 'Shout At The Devil' *et al*. Although Nikki's lyricism is as acute and damning as ever, somehow there is little sharpness or shape to the whole affair. It is not a record likely to last the course of time.

That seems to be the general feeling of most Mötley fans. The LP is something of a flop in the US, UK and almost everywhere else. Traditional fans of the band don't appreciate this change in direction, whilst younger fans want bands of their own generation – new heroes, not hand-me-down ones. Mötley's prior reputation as a glam band still sticks rigidly with them, despite Nikki's protests to Sylvie:

"We haven't been a glam band for years. We kind of dumped all that when it reached its peak of popularity, and there are so many bands that were copying us, and we just left it in the dust with 'Girls, Girls, Girls'."

Just after the album is released, Tommy runs into his own troubles when he's fined $200 after being caught at Los Angeles Airport with a concealed gun (a .40

calibre shotgun, no less) on his person. But Nikki has better news in store, when on April 14, Brandi gives birth to their second child – a daughter, Storm Brieanne.

"I delivered her myself!" says the proud father, who takes six weeks pre-tour paternity leave to be with his wife and baby. When Sylvie ran into Nikki and his very pregnant wife shortly before at a children's birthday party at Steve Vai's house, he was playing ball with son Gunnar and extolling the joys of fatherhood and family. It had changed his life, he said – absolutely for the better.

Mötley plan to begin their tour duties (a trek they dub the 'Anywhere There's Electricity' tour) with a performance at a biker festival in Wyoming in front of some 300,000 Hell's Angels.

"Tommy and I ride with a lot of the Hell's Angels in Los Angeles, and they invited us to play in this huge dirt field," Nikki tells *RAW*.

Touring proper is scheduled to start during mid-June in Phoenix – an arena tour to put Mötley firmly back at the very top. It proves to be a disaster.

East Coast US dates have originally been booked with The Ramones, the Butthole Surfers, Kings X and the Bad Livers ("They're a Stray Cats type band, who do Metallica, AC/DC and Black Sabbath covers," Nikki enthuses about the last-named) the preferred support acts.

"We want to do a five-hour show that's really bizarre," Nikki tells Dave Ling. In the end, though, The Ramones and the Butthole Surfers fail to resolve an argument over their respective billing, and both pull off the tour. Mötley have to settle for the talented trio Kings X (critics' faves, yet not crowd pullers), dark goths Type O Negative, controversial sado-masochists The Genitorturers and southern boogie band Brother Cane – and prospective ticket sales are so bad that they are forced to move gigs into smaller venues, and then to cancel many of them altogether!

Mötley's fan base, it would seem, has inexplicably collapsed. The 'Motley Crue' album disappears from the Top 200 in the US after just three months and barely scrapes sales figures of half-a-million (ie gold status). To put this into perspective, 'Dr. Feelgood' sold in excess of four million copies in America alone!

But, Nikki is in defiant mood when he confronts journalist Steffan Chirazi:

"Like any songwriter, like any band we're growing and developing. We set a precedent for a lot of bands. We broke the rules as we went along as much as we wanted to... Now that we're out playing theatres and the like, it reminds me of 'Shout At The Devil'. It's unbelievable. We're back in buses. It's so much fun. We're seeing things, we're living again.

"Before, it was so big it was scary. All those limos. Me and Tommy HATE limos! We used to fight all the time about why we couldn't have a beat-up old van to take us places! Why we have to have security guys everywhere, jets. Vince had to have limos. We rode in the luggage van nearly every day because we were dying to be real. I wanted the success of the band, of course, but you don't want that particular dream to come true, because it's ugly.

"I remember seeing the Stones at the Toronto Skydome Stadium. I felt sorry for them! Man, I bet they'd shoot their mother in the back to play where we're playing tonight. Look it was a great time, but it turned into everything we rebelled against... We were a machine.

"The new album is very selfish. Not a lot of people can get in. Only the diehards will find a way. We did everything in our power to make a non-pop hit album. The concept of the 'hit album' made us sick to our stomachs. We knew we'd end up being thrust into a land of over-exposure again.

"If this album had sold 20 million copies, I'd feel fuckin' amazed, but I don't expect it to. My self-esteem is not based on album sales or concert tickets, but I'm a bit of a fucked-up personality. I'd rather play theatres than arenas."

All this palaver leads some people, inevitably, to speculate as to whether a reunion with Vince and a return to the victorious Mötley Crüe of old might be just around the corner, Nikki's protestations about hating the trappings of success notwithstanding. However, when this subject is mooted by MTV during an interview with Nikki, the bassist is none too amused. And when the same interviewer asks for Nikki's reaction to the fact that Mötley's former singer had recently been injured in a jet-ski accident whilst doing a promotional stunt for his swimwear line, the bassist responds with the curt line that he was more concerned with how much damage "300lbs of blubber" might do to the coastline (a reference to the fact that Neil had put on some considerable weight since leaving the Crüe and coming off the road).

Vince himself isn't having the best of years. Forced to cancel touring plans because of those throat problems, he spends the early part of '94 with a residency every Tuesday night at the Bar One club in Hollywood. Called Vince Neil's 'Ruby Tuesdays', the singer gets to jam with various local musicians in a band called Vince Neil's All-Stars.

He does a 20-minute set each Tuesday before a couple of hundred fans, charging an entrance fee of $15 for kids to hear the likes of 'Dr. Feelgood', 'Girls, Girls, Girls', 'Kickstart My Heart' and 'Sister Of Pain'.

However, in the Summer, Vince (now managing himself) is back in the studio working on a second album for Warner Brothers, with the much-vaunted and sought-after team of The Dust Brothers acting as producers.

Considering that their previous client roster includes the likes of hardcore rapper Ice T and the Beastie Boys one can only wait and wonder precisely what Vince will unleash.

By this time, Stevens has returned to Billy Idol's band (so much for the Neil-Stevens alliance being as significant and influential as had been the David Lee Roth/Steve Vai partnership). Dave Marshall becomes the sole guitarist in the Vince Neil Band. This record should be out in 1995.

But Nikki's reaction in the summer to the idea of Mötley and Vince cutting their losses and embracing each other once more still hasn't mellowed.

"He *(Vince)* was a carcass of a used-to-be-young rebel," he tells *RAW*. "He was into it for all the wrong reasons. To tell Vince we wanted to deflate our own career, play smaller places and do an album that was anti-commercial, he'd think we were fucking crazy. There's a Ferrari payment to be made.

"I don't mean to slag Vince. I'm only speaking the truth. Right now, we're enjoying playing. We're losing thousand of dollars on the road because we're having fun.

"But we wish that cat all the luck in the world. I hope he gets to be as big as Michael Jackson, but I wouldn't wish to be that big on any terms, except my own. In retrospect, we've had some great times together, but those times are now gone. Vince was the one who wanted to be a rock star. We all wanted to be dead!"

As the end of '94 approaches, the glorious Mötley Crüe cavalcade has all but run out of steam. So, what does the future hold for the band and their erstwhile vocalist?

Chapter Thirteen
Time for Change

In the late '80s, it really did seem that all you needed to do was hang around the right places in LA in the right clothes to get a major recording contract. Fuelled by the ever-greedy beast that was MTV, a succession of bands – some good, others not so – sold huge quantities of records. Platinum albums were as commonplace in LA as flaking skin in a leper colony. The bandwagon, it seemed, was perpetual in its magnetic motion.

But something happened in the early '90s. Young rock fans turned their back on LA and the frivolity and brain-dead superficiality of the glam scene it had spawned. Maybe, it was because there was too much rubbish being churned out, or perhaps it was simply the wheel of fate taking a much-needed turn in a different direction. Whatever, the platinum started to fade, reality turning it to rust as a new breed of more down to earth, serious and extreme bands began to dominate. Nirvana, Pearl Jam, Alice In Chains, Soundgarden, Nine Inch Nails. They and bands like them were the new aristocracy – building a new world order on the rubble which was all that remained of the stilettos, lipgloss and spandex of the old establishment.

In their wake, erstwhile icons were pulled off pedestals, kicking and screaming, yet emphatically consigned to the metaphorical dumper. Poison, Warrant, David Lee Roth – they all found themselves ignored and branded as irrelevant. Vince Neil, too, felt that cold wind rushing in when he released 'Exposed'. And Mötley followed suit, into virtual oblivion.

Mötley's demise is arguably the most stunning and shocking of them all. David Lee Roth had been in gradual decline for years. Poison and Warrant were comparative over-achievers who had succeeded to some degree because they imitated what was once irrefutably the most commercial form of rock'n'roll in America – '80s Mötley music.

But to see the originators themselves (the godfathers of the LA scene) come off the rails so comprehensively was truly amazing to behold. Maybe they'd made the mistake of trying to adapt all too openly to contemporary trends. Perhaps the unedifying row between Neil and the Crüe conducted in the media alienated fans from both parties. Certainly, young kids just cutting their teeth on rock music felt the Crüe to be anachronistic. And, taking into account the ever-biting economic recession, 'Motley Crue' probably had little chance. It was a lead weight ostrich trying to fly – forget it!

145

So, what next? Will Mötley and Vince, flops apart from each other, bury their differences and reunite? Despite the protestations to the contrary and the poisoned barbs aimed by both, don't bet against this happening, albeit not for a while. It wouldn't be the first time that warring factions have embraced for the 'greater good'. But, with Vince planning a second solo album, and Mötley seemingly ever more determined to pursue their preferred musical direction – whatever the suicidal commercial cost – a reunion might be some way off just at the moment.

But what does Nikki make of the current LA scene, one that has changed so much since the halcyon days of the early-to-mid '80s?

"I don't know," he told Sylvie. "I haven't been to a club in years. I've lost interest. I have a studio in my house and I just sit in my studio and make music and that's it. I work out, I run. I spend time with my wife and my kids. I have a bunch of friends, me and Tommy ride with some of the Hell's Angels out in the Valley, we go on runs up to San Francisco on our bikes and stuff, but otherwise I make music. In between doing work, family, work, family... I haven't had a life in a couple of years at least."

Tommy: "I still see the glam bands bubbling around. Warrant and Winger still have an influence... But I DON'T see originality. When we came out there was no-one else as weird. No-one else was doing their hair up to here."

Seattle and the sound it spawned – grunge – now dictates and dominates. Nikki, as a native of that fair (and rainy) city, has his views on that scene as well:

"I think there are a couple of good bands there. I like what Nirvana did... I like Alice In Chains a whole lot. I prefer the bands that are a little more raw than Pearl Jam or something. They don't move me. It's like 'grunge light' or something.

"We're not trying to fit in. I'm not going to start wearing flannels or growing a goatee. That's not me. It's not Mötley Crüe. To me, we've always been a hard rock version of David Bowie, in that we've always evolved and emerged as something totally new and fresh... I pride myself on change... Anyway, the stuff out there isn't that great. I go out and buy a hundred CDs at a time, then I hook myself up and listen to all of them. I get very disappointed, there are only a few great songs. The other seven just don't cut it in my book.

"I'm not putting down the bands of the '90s, but for every Pearl Jam there are five dozen bands trying to copy them. People put down the '80s 'cos a lot of bands just copied one another and that was true, but it's true now as well."

Perhaps Nikki is deluding himself slightly when he compares Mötley to Bowie. If the Crüe changed from album to album, then this was via an evolutionary

process. The change from 'Dr. Feelgood' to 'Motley Crue' was revolutionary – and Mötley fans simply do not seem to want such a radical upheaval. Bowie made his name through controlled upheaval. The same is not true of Mötley.

The question of what comes next is one that must be troubling the band. There is more than their musical credibility to consider. That $25 million contract with Elektra should ensure that the record label will bring pressure to bear on Mötley to snap back into commercial gear and take a safer path to restoring their diminishing fortunes. Only time will tell how this situation will resolve itself. Do Mötley go straight out and make another album to prove that they are following the right musical path, thereby risking the prospect of taking another bath? Or will they consider even splitting up, or opening negotiations with Vince Neil for a return that many people privately feel to be their only logical option? Should be interesting to see.

Meantime, there is another Mötley record already completed. It is to be released in the late Summer of '94 throughout America and Canada. This is an EP titled 'Leftovers'. It features one solo track from each current member of the band and, says John, "Will be sold through mail order initially. This stuff is really cool, 'cos you're able to hear everybody's influences."

Nikki: "I told Bob Rock that I wanted to do something a bit different, although I didn't want to do anything that would take the wind out of Mötley Crüe's sails, 'cos that's first and foremost. However, I do see myself branching and doing something similar, maybe a side band too – but it'd all be done with the consent of my brothers, so to speak."

Nikki's 'Leftovers' contribution was recorded with a member of Canadian techno-industrial combo Front Line Assembly. As for Tommy...
"My thing is more of a house, industrial, techno affair... I made my thing primarily for it to be played in clubs, for people to dance to." Tommy plays everything himself on this track.

Mick's is a more traditional instrumental: "It has no title. It's a blues piece, slow – but isn't a three-chord, cry-in-your-beer type thing. It will give people a chance to hear where my roots are: Beck, Page, Hendrix... If I were ever to do something other than Mötley Crüe, I'd take (singers) John Corabi, Glenn Hughes, (soul man) Aaron Neville, the horn section from Tower Of Power and (drummer) Tony Thompson (Powerstation/Crown Of Thorns). It'd be a heavy blues progression deal... I'd do it just for the fun of it."

IMPORTED

100 PROOF

Rumple Minze

PEPPERMINT SCHNAPPS

149

When 'Leftovers' finally sees the light of day in the UK and Europe remains to be seen. Nikki has spoken about putting on some live cuts and studio out-takes and developing 'Leftovers' into a full-blown album for these markets. In the meantime, there must be a severe question mark hanging over the Mötleys' immediate future. The record book shows that once a band goes into decline, then it's unusual for that slide to be arrested.

Nikki claims that this doesn't bother him...

"My heroes don't sell records. The Sisters Of Mercy don't sell records. Iggy Pop doesn't sell records. The Stooges never sold records. It doesn't bother me. And if you wanna talk about playing the clubs, that's where Cheap Trick are these days – I think that's cool!"

Whether this is truly Nikki's state of mind – or just an attempt to come to terms with the harsh reality of the Mötley situation in '94 can only be speculated upon. Only he knows the truth.

Mötley Crüe have given so much entertainment to so many millions over the past 13 years that it would be tragic to see them merely disintegrate and become an embittered parody of themselves. Yet, whatever the future might hold for them, let's hope it doesn't tarnish the past.

For all the pleasure they've given since 1981, all we can say in conclusion is: THANKS!

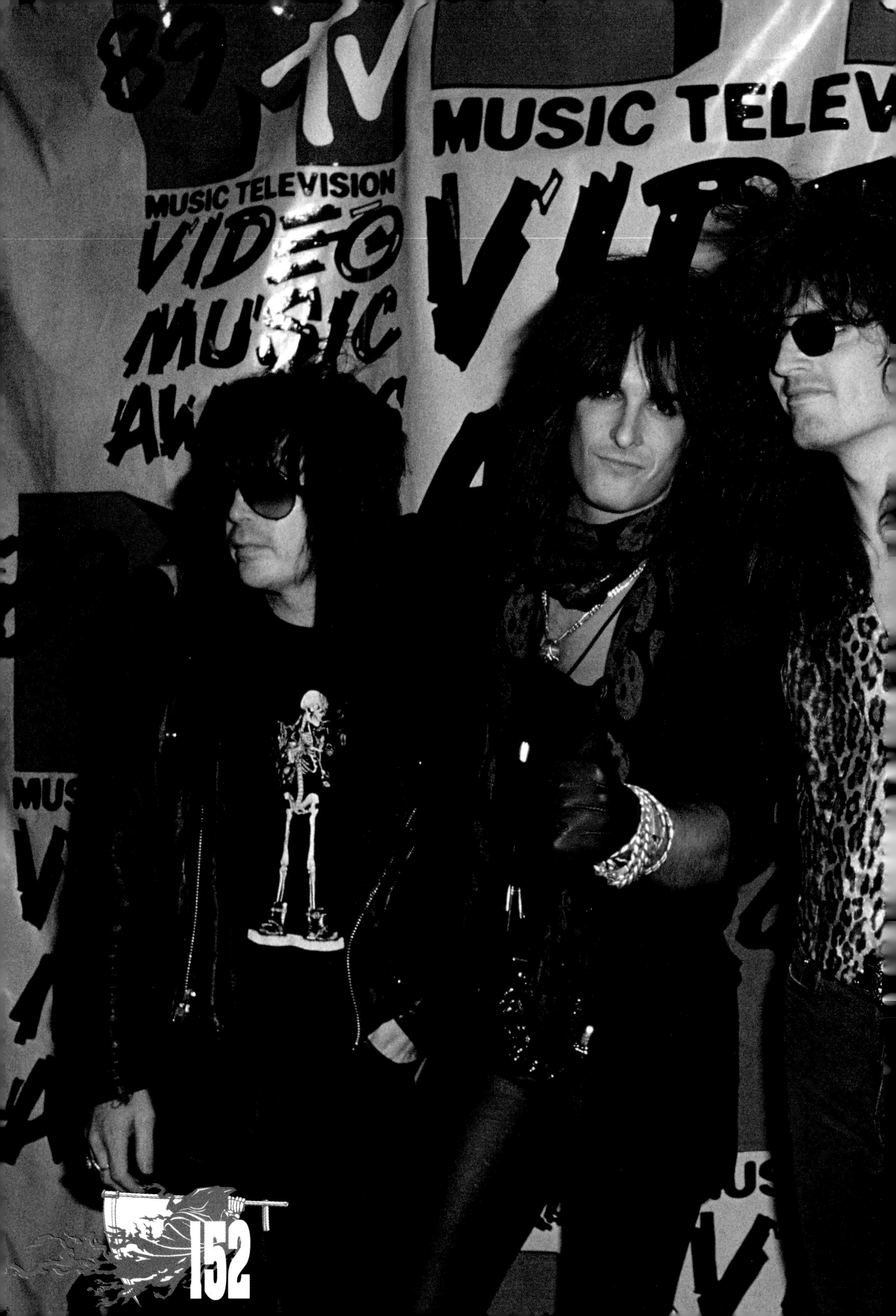
'89 MTV
MUSIC TELEVISION
VIDEO
MUSIC

153

Epilögue – by Malcolm Dome

unset Strip is mournfully quiet these days. Dust has settled grimly on the theatrical and dazzling hopes which once attracted young musicians from all parts of America, from all manner of backgrounds, unified in their belief that they could be the next band to emulate the meteoric rise of Mötley Crüe.

LA glam metal connects the hedonistic, seemingly gratuitous days of stadium rock in the '70s with the altogether more serious acumen of the '90s. The scene re-established a sense of fun, being arguably as important in the pin-pricking of rock's pomposity as had been the British punk era a few years previously.

But is there any place now for such bands in a decade dominated by the caring, sharing philosophy of a culture increasingly scared of the ramifications of excess? As one looks at the way Mötley's contemporaries (Ratt, Great White, Dokken, Quiet Riot, WASP) have fallen apart and disappeared without ready replacements taking their place, it is easy to become despondent about the genre's capacity for survival.

But, rock'n'roll should – indeed, must – maintain a place in its heart for those who perceive it as an entertainment form, for those who wish to lighten the burden of life. The Los Angeles glam scene might seem at the moment to be an artefact of a bygone age, but it will rise again.

It may take a few years to accomplish, but the legacy of Mötley Crüe and their ilk will inspire a future generation of decadent, outrageous lotharios. Sunset Strip will once again thrum with the life force of bands demanding a 'piece of your action'. Bet on it!

155

Appendix A: Album discography

'Too Fast For Love' (Leathür Records – 1982): 'Live Wire' / 'Come On And Dance' / 'Public Enemy No. 1' / 'Merry Go Round' / 'Take Me To The Top' / 'Piece Of Your Action' / 'Sleazy Eyes' / 'Too Fast For Love' / 'On With The Show' / 'Stick To Your Guns'.

'Too Fast For Love' (Elektra K 52425 – 1982): 'Live Wire' / 'Come On And Dance' / 'Public Enemy No. 1' / 'Merry Go Round' / 'Take Me To The Top' / 'Piece Of Your Action' / 'Sleazy Eyes' / 'Too Fast For Love' / 'On With The Show'.

'Shout At The Devil' (Elektra 7559-60289-2 – 1983): 'In The Beginning' / 'Shout At The Devil' / 'Looks That Kill' / 'Bastard' / 'God Bless The Children Of The Beast' / 'Helter Skelter' / 'Red Hot' / 'Too Young To Fall In Love' / 'Knock 'Em Dead Kid' / 'Ten Seconds To Love' / 'Danger'.

'Theatre Of Pain' (Elektra 7559-60418-2 – 1985): 'City Boy Blues' / 'Smokin' In The Boys' Room' / 'Louder Than Hell' / 'Keep Your Eye On The Money' / 'Home Sweet Home' / 'Tonight (We Need A Lover' / 'Use It Or Lose It' / 'Save Our Souls' / 'Raise Your Hands To Rock' / 'Fight For Your Rights'.

'Girls, Girls, Girls' (Elektra 7559-60725-2 – 1987): 'Wild Side' / 'Girls, Girls, Girls' / 'Dancin' On Glass' / 'Bad Boy Boogie' / 'Nona' / 'Five Years Dead' / 'All In The Name Of...' / 'Sumthin' For Nuthin' / 'You're All I Need' / 'Jailhouse Rock'.

'Dr. Feelgood' (Elektra 7559-60829-2 – 1989): 'T.n.T. (Terror 'n Tinseltown)' / 'Dr. Feelgood' / 'Slice Of Your Pie' / 'Rattlesnake Shake' / 'Kickstart My Heart' / 'Without You' / 'Same Ol' Situation (S.O.S.)' / 'Sticky Sweet' / 'She Goes Down' / 'Don't Go Away Mad (Just Go Away)' / 'Time For Change'.

'Decade Of Decadence' (Elektra EKT95 – 1991): 'Live Wire' / 'Piece Of Your Action' / 'Shout At The Devil' / 'Looks That Kill' / 'Home Sweet Home' / 'Smokin' In The Boys' Room' / 'Girls, Girls, Girls' / 'Wild Side' / 'Dr. Feelgood' / 'Kickstart My Heart' / 'Teaser' / 'Rock'N'Roll Junkie' / 'Primal Scream' / 'Angela' / 'Anarchy In The UK'.

'Motley Crue' (Elektra 7559-61534-2 – 1994): 'Power To The Music' / 'Uncle Jack' / 'Hooligan's Holiday' / 'Misunderstood' / 'Loveshine' / 'Poison Apples' / 'Hammered' / 'Til Death Do Us Part' / 'Welcome To The Numb' / 'Smoke The Sky' / 'Droppin' Like Flies' / 'Driftaway'.

158

Appendix B: Photographic Index